"On the Indian Trail"

And Other Stories of Missionary Work Among the Cree
and Saulteaux Indians

by Reverend Egerton Ryerson Young

(1840-1909)

CONTENTS:

# PREFACE:

This is not a continuous narrative of missionary work as are some of the author's books. It is a collection of distinct chapters, some of which are written expressly for this volume, others of which, having in whole or in part seen the light in other form, are now, at the request of friends, and thanks to the courtesy of the publishers, here gathered.

Romantic missionary work among the red Indians will soon be a thing of the past. Civilisation is reaching this people, and the iron horse rushes and shrieks where the Indian trail was once the only pathway. The picturesque garb is fast disappearing, and store clothes, often too soon transformed into rags anything but picturesque, have robbed, the Indian of the interest that once clung to him.

These wanderings on the fast disappearing trail, speak of successes rather than failures; not but that there were many of the latter, as well as long waiting after the seed time for the harvest, but because it is so much more pleasant and helpful to look on the bright side of life, and talk of victory rather than defeat.

So in the hope that this book will be helpful and encouraging to the friends and supporters of missions, who have become such an innumerable company, and that His name may be glorified thereby, we send it on its way.

E.R.Y. Toronto.

Chapter One.

On the Prairie Trail.

We struck the prairie trail at Saint Paul in 1868.

We, that is my young wife and I in company with some
other missionaries and teachers, were to travel many
hundreds of miles upon it, in order that we might reach the
wigwam haunts of the Indians in the northern part of the
Hudson Bay Territories, to whom we had been appointed to
carry the glorious Gospel of the Son of God.

We were to follow up the work begun by men of sublime
faith and heroic courage, and to carry it still farther into
more remote regions where as yet the sweet story of a
Saviour's love had never been heard. We had confidence
enough in God to belief that if fur-traders could travel
along these trails, and live in those lonely remote regions
for from the blessings of civilisation, and in order to make
money by trading with the Indians put up with the
hardships and privations incident to such a life, we could
make equal sacrifices for Christ's sake, to carry the Glad
Tidings of His great love to those who had never heard the
wondrous Story.

After about three weeks journeyings, we had travelled as
far as we could by steamboat and railroad, and were at the
extreme limit of these splendid methods of civilised
locomotion. From this point onward there was nothing
before us but the prairie trail. On and on it stretched for
hundreds of miles, away and away to the land of the north
wind. Over its winding undulating course, long years ago,
the hardy pioneers of the new world adventured

themselves; and as they bravely pushed on they were filled with amazement and awe at the vastness of the great and illimitable prairies.

Following closely in their trail, and even sometimes themselves the pioneers, came those early heroic priestly followers of Loyola, eager and anxious to meet and to make friends of the wild Indians of the plains and forest, that among them they might plant the cross, and, according to their belief, by the simple rite of baptism induct them into the bosom of Mother Church.

In later years much of the romance of the great Trail had worn away. Commerce and Trade with their multiplied activities had so taken possession of it that when first we saw it in 1868, the long trains of noisy creaking Red River carts, and the great canvas-covered wagons of the adventurous immigrants, were the most conspicuous sights on its dusty stretches. Occasionally bands of Indian warriors, plumed and painted, were seen upon it, dashing along on their fiery steeds, out on some marauding adventure, or more likely, on the lookout for the vast herds of buffalo that still swarmed in the regions farther west, like "the cattle on a thousand hills."

It was one of those perfect days in the lovely month of June when we left the thriving young city of Saint Paul, and with our canvas-covered wagons, and fourteen picked horses, really entered on the trail. As we left the frontier city, thus severing the last link that bound us to civilisation, we realised most vividly that now we were entering upon our missionary work.

Thirty days were we on this Prairie Trail. Not all of them were of that rare beauty of the first. Fierce thunderstorms several times assailed us when it was not always possible to protect ourselves from the terrible downpour of rain. One night a genuine cyclone wrecked our camp; tents and wagons with their varied contents went careering in erratic courses before its irresistible power.

Our way was beset with dangers: bridgeless streams had to be crossed; prairie fires had to be fought, or wildly run away from treacherous quicksands sometimes spread most invitingly on either side of the miserable looking trail, lured the unwary traveller to trust himself on their smooth and shining surface. But woe to the foolish ones who left the trail for the quicksands: unless speedily rescued by the united strength of friends, horses and travellers would soon be swallowed up; so the warning cry of the guide was ever: "Keep in the trail!"

Thus we journeyed on, sometimes in the sunshine, and sometimes in the storm. Every morning and evening we had our family prayers. The Sabbaths were rest days for all—sweet and precious days, when out in the sunshine on the glorious prairies, we, a little company of missionaries and teachers—worshipped God: they were as the days of the Son of Man on earth.

Thirty days on such a trail could not pass without some strange adventures, and we had our share of them with white men and with Indians.

A talkative parrot in our party nearly frightened the lives out of some very inquisitive and superstitious Indians and French half-breeds. They had stopped their ox-carts one day at the same spot where we, coming in the opposite direction, were resting for the dinner hour. Hearing about the wonderful parrot, they crowded around to see her. Polly stood their inquisitive gazings for awhile, then, apparently somewhat annoyed, with wings ruffled, sprang forward as far as she could in her large cage, and shouted out:

"Who are you?"

The effect upon the superstitious half-breeds, and Indians, was about as though His Satanic Majesty had suddenly appeared among them. They rushed away, and nothing that we could do would induce any of them to look at the bird again.

Another adventure, most unique and startling, occurred on this trip ere we had proceeded many days on the trail.

"You had better keep a sharp eye on those splendid horses of yours, or you may wake up some fine morning and find them missing."

This was rather startling news and caused a good deal of excitement in our camp.

The speakers were some scouts from the United States army, who were making a hurried trip from the head waters of the Missouri where the troops had gone to quell some Indian disturbance. They were now on their way to Saint Paul with dispatches for Washington.

Each night of our journey we had, in true western style hobbled our horses and left them to roam about and feed on the luxuriant grasses. This hobbling is merely the tying of the forefeet loosely together with soft leather thongs so that the animal in moving has to lift up both forefeet at once. Its movements being thus necessarily slow, there is no roaming very far from the camp. Having had no fear of danger, we had been very careless, leaving everything unguarded.

The terrible Sioux massacres a few years before in these very regions, were now being forgotten. It is true that as we journeyed, the ruins of the destroyed, and in many places, not yet rebuilt homesteads of the settlers, were vivid reminders of those dreadful frontier wars, when over nine hundred white people lost their lives. The Indians were now however far to the north and west of us, so that we had no fears as we leisurely moved along. Hence, it was somewhat startling when these picturesquely garbed scouts halted in our midst, and warned us to have a guard over our horses; telling us, that, the most notorious band of horse thieves was in the neighbourhood, and was rumoured to have heard that there was a party with some magnificent horses in the prairie country, and that doubtless, even now, they were on the lookout for us upon some of the trails.

After a short halt for a hurried meal, our bronzed well-armed visitors left us. The last we saw of them was as they galloped away southward on the trail.

Immediately a council was called, when it was decided to move on to the vicinity of Clearwater, and there remain until all the final preparations for our long trip were completed. Our horses were turned loose and hobbled during the day, but were not allowed to stray very far from the camp. Watchful eyes were ever upon them, and also scanning the prairies for suspicious intruders. Before sundown they were all gathered in and securely fastened in a large barn that stood out upon the prairie, the sole building left of a large farmstead: all the other buildings, including the dwelling house, had been burned during the Indian wars. No survivors or relatives had as yet come to claim the deserted place, and so the rich prairie grasses had almost covered with their green verdure the spot where the destroyed buildings once stood; and now all that remained to tell of former prosperity was this solitary old barn.

The men of our party were appointed to watch the barn during the night and protect the horses against all intruders. Two well armed persons were thought a sufficient guard for each of the eight or ten nights that we remained in that vicinity. One night a young man of our party and I were appointed to watch. He most thoroughly equipped himself with several varieties of weapons, resolved to be prepared for any emergency. I trusted to a quick-firing breech-loading rifle.

We gathered in the horses from the prairies, and were leading them toward the barn when we met the leader of our party, a man past middle life, most of whose years had been spent among the Indians, and in the great west.

Looking at us who were to be the guards of the horses that night, he said, with a sneer:

"Queer guards are you! I have some young Indians that could steal any horse in that crowd to-night from under your very nose."

Stung by the sneers of this man, for it was not the first time that he had tried to wound, I replied with perhaps too much emphasis:

"Mr — I have the best horse in the company, and I will give him to you, if either you, or any Indian living, can steal him out of that barn between sundown and sunrise."

My comrade and I carefully fastened our horses along one side of the barn where they could stand comfortably, or lie down on some old prairie hay during the night. Then we examined the barn. At one end were the usual large double doors sufficiently wide and high to admit of the entrance of a wagon loaded with hay or sheaves of grain. At the other end was a small door which we securely fastened on the inside. We then carefully examined the building for other places of ingress to make sure that there were no openings sufficiently large for even a naked savage to squeeze through. When thoroughly satisfied with our survey, we collected a quantity of dried hay, and made ourselves some comfortable seats, where we could, without being seen, command the large end doors: one of which was fastened inside with a hook and staple, while the other had only the usual wooden latch.

We moved about and chatted on various subjects during the long beautiful gloaming, and when the darkness settled down upon us, we made ourselves comfortable in our assigned positions, and with rides in hand, were indeed sentinels on the watch. As the excitement of the occasion wore off, my young companion who was still in his teens, began to feel exceedingly drowsy. I told him to cuddle down in the hay and go to sleep for a while, and if there was any appearance of danger I would instantly awake him. Very soon he was sleeping quietly at my feet. He had generously requested me to awake him when he had slept an hour or so, offering then to take my place. Thanking him, I said: "Get some sleep if you can; there is none, however, for me to-night."—I remembered too well those taunting words, and could not have slept had I tried.

As the hours slowly rolled along, I could not but think of the strange transitions of the last few weeks. Not six weeks before this I was the pastor of a large church in a flourishing city. Then I was living in a beautiful home with all the comforts and conveniences of civilisation around me, where the vigilant policemen paced their various rounds, while we in peace and safety rested without one thought of danger; now I was in the far West, away from the society and comforts of other days, on the boundless plains where dangers lurk, and lawless, thievish vagabonds abound. Not long ago I was in my own pulpit preaching to large congregations; now, during the quiet hours of this night, I was sitting on a bundle of dried prairie grass in an old barn, defending a lot of horses from horse thieves. Strange transformations are these. Truly life is a play, and we, the actors, little know what parts we shall next be called on to assume.

Thus I mused; bub hush! What noise is that? Surely it cannot be that a cunning horse thief would come so deliberately this beautiful starlit night and try at the principal door to seek an entrance. No stealthy Indian clever at horse stealing would begin his operations in such a way.

But there is the sound, nevertheless. Evidently it is that of a hand feeling for the latch.

Strict orders had been given at the camp, that under no consideration should any one of our party approach the barn after dark. So, here was an intruder who must be promptly dealt with, before he could draw and fire.

Springing up and lifting the rifle to my shoulder, I waited until the intruder's hand had found the latch. Then the door swung open and there he stood; a very tall man, clearly outlined in the starry night.

My first grim resolve was to fire at once. Then there came the thought: "It is a terrible thing suddenly to send a soul into eternity. Perhaps he is not a horse thief. He may be some lone wanderer on the prairies, who, seeing this old barn, desires to get under its shelter out of the heavy dews. You have him covered with your rifle; even if he is a desperate horse thief bent on mischief, ere he can draw his weapons, you can easily drop him."

These thoughts must have flashed through my brains very rapidly for the man had not yet entered the barn when I had decided on my course of action.

So, while keeping him covered with my rifle, and with my hand upon the trigger, I shouted:

"Who's there?"

"It's only Matthew. Surely you ought to know me by this time."

Instead of an enemy, there came stumbling along in the darkness, one of our young friends from the camp: a school-teacher, going out to instruct the Indians in the plains of the Saskatchewan.

Groping his way along, he said: "It is awfully close and hot down there in the camp, and so I thought I would rather come and spend the rest of the night with you in the barn."

Foolish fellow! he little knew how near he had come to losing his life by this direct breach of orders.

As I recognised his voice in answer to my challenge, and realised how near I had come to shooting one of our party, a quick reaction seized me, and dropping the gun, I sank back trembling like a leaf.

After chatting away at a great rate, he at length settled down in the hay, and went to sleep without having the slightest idea of the risk he had run, or of the part I had played in what came so near being a tragedy.

I continued my watch until relieved at sunrise, and then, with my comrade, turned over all the horses safe and sound to those whose duty it was to watch them while they were feeding on the prairies.

There was a row for a time when I reported to the leaders of our company the visit to the barn. The good-natured delinquent was the subject of a great deal of scolding, which he bore with an unruffled demeanour. As he was six feet, six inches and a half in stature, no physical castigation was administered; nor was any needed; he was so thoroughly frightened when he heard how he had stood under cover of my rifle with my finger on the trigger.

Chapter Two.

On the Indian Trail.

We will call the routes over which I travelled on my large
mission field, "Indian trails;" but the name at times would
be found to be inept, as often, for scores of miles, there was
not the least vestige of a track or path. This was because
there was so little travel in summer of a character that
would make a well defined trail, for during that season the
Indians preferred to avail themselves of the splendid and
numerous lakes and rivers, which enabled them to travel
very easily by canoe in almost any direction.

Thus, when obliged to travel on the short stretches of the
so-called, "Indian trail," it is not to be wondered at if the
missionary sometimes lost his way, and had to be sought
after and found, much to the amusement of the Indians who
constituted the hunting party.

"Good missionary, but him lost the trail." More than once
was I so addressed by my clever and experienced Indian
canoeman, with whom every summer I used to journey
hundreds of miles into remote regions, to find the poor
sheep of the wilderness to whom to preach the glorious
Gospel of the Son of God. These summer routes lay
through many lakes, and up and down rushing rivers full of
rapids and cataracts. Generally two skilful Indian
canoemen were my companions, one of whom was called,
"the guide."

The Indians, for whom we were seeking, drifted naturally
from their hunting grounds in the forests, to the shores of
the lakes and rivers, for the sake of the fish, which, daring

the summer months, could be easily obtained and which then constituted their principal food. The result was, that while in winter, with our dog-trains, we could go anywhere—the terrible ice-king freezing everything solid from the lakes and rivers to the great quaking bogs—in summer, we were confined to those trips which could be only made by the birch-bark canoe: in no other way could the Gospel he carried to these people. After we became accustomed to the canoe and dog-train, we rejoiced that we were counted worthy to be the Messengers of Good Tidings' to these neglected ones, who, having lost faith in their old paganism, were longing for something better.

One summer in the early years of my missionary life, when I had had but little experience in the northern methods of travel and was a novice at finding my way on an obscure trail, I took a trip which I remember very distinctly; partly, because of the difficulty I had in keeping the trail when alone and partly because of the dangers to which I was exposed when I lost it.

My birch canoe was a good one. It was made especially for running rapids, and was so light that one man could easily carry it on his head when necessary. I had as my companions two very capable Indian canoemen. One of them had never been over that route before and the other, whom by courtesy, we called, "our guide," had only once travelled that way—and that, several years before the date of this trip.

All the able bodied men of my mission excepting these two, were away serving the Hudson Bay Company as tripmen, which was the reason why I could not obtain men better acquainted with the long route. I had either to take these men and ran a good deal of risk, or wait another year to carry the Gospel to those hundreds who had never heard it, and who had sent a pleading call for me to come and tell them what the Great Spirit said in His Book. So, after much prayer, I decided, trusting in God and in these men, to make the journey.

The country through which we travelled was one of the roughest and wildest in that dreary, desolate land. The streams were so full of rapids that we had constantly to be making portages. This was slow and laborious work. Our method of procedure was something like this: as soon as we discovered that the current was too rapid to be safe, or that we were hearing some great falls, we went ashore and quickly unloaded our canoe; William, the guide, easily lifted it upon his head and starting off, soon disappeared in the forest, running where possible, and keeping parallel with the raging stream until he reached a place below which the waters were again navigable; Peter, my other Indian, as speedily as possible made a large bundle of our blankets, kettles, and supplies, and with this upon his back, supported by a carrying strap round his forehead, quickly followed the trail made by William; while to me was assigned the work of carrying the guns, ammunition, changes of raiment and the presents, and Bibles for the Indians we expected to visit. Although my load was not nearly as heavy as those carried by my stalwart canoemen, yet I was utterly unable to keep up with them in the trail. Indians, when thus loaded, never walk: they seem to glide along on a swinging trot that carries them over the ground very rapidly. A white man, unaccustomed to this pace, is very soon left behind. This was my experience. All I could do, was to trudge bravely along under my miscellaneous load, which was becoming constantly disarranged, thus causing delay.

But my greatest trouble was to keep the trail. There was absolutely no path. All the trail, was that made by my two Indians, and Indians are trained to leave as little evidence of their movements as possible. So I was often lost. I would at the beginning of the portage, bravely shoulder my burden and endeavour to keep in sight of my men. This, however, I found to be an utter impossibility. A sharp turn among the rocky ridges, or a plunge into the dense dark forest, and they were gone from my vision. Then my perplexities began. If, as some times happened, the trail was through mud, or reeds and rushes I could generally follow them in it; but, as more frequently happened, the trail was over rocky ridges, or through dense forests, sometimes for miles, and I was often completely bewildered and lost.

The trouble at first was, that being too perplexed, or too ignorant of what was the safer course to pursue, I would quicken my pace and hurry on—somewhere. On and on I would stumble under my heavy awkward load until the sweat fell like rain from my brow and my back ached. More than once when thus hurrying I have been startled by some savage beast, that with a snort or a growl, dashed away in front of me. This only added speed to my footsteps, and frightened now I would hurry on, until utterly worn-out and exhausted I threw off my heavy burdens and sank down on the nearest rock or log, tired out. Perhaps in my ignorance and perversity I had wandered far away, even in an opposite direction from that which I should have taken.

Fortunate was it for me that I had such men for my comrades. I knew their worth and loyalty, as well as their ability quickly to find me. As soon as they had safely reached the end of the portage they would be on the alert for my arrival. If I delayed beyond what they thought to be sufficient time they would set off on the back trail looking for me. With that unerring instinct which so many of them possess in woodcraft, and which to me always seemed perfectly marvellous, they soon found where I had wandered from the trail. From this point they had not the slightest difficulty in following and finding me. Without any chiding, but with perhaps a pitying look and a quiet utterance that sounded like "Good missionary, but him lost the trail," they would quickly pick up my burdens, and safely guide me to our waiting canoe. All I had to carry was perhaps the Book which I had with me, the reading of which, enabled me profitably to pass the hours that often elapsed ere my faithful men found me.

We lived on just what we could shoot, as it was impossible to carry additional supplies in a birch canoe. Hunter's luck varies considerably even in a land of game, and we at least had variety in our bill of fare. Black bears being still numerous in those wild regions we sometimes had bear's steak broiled on the coals, or ribs skidded on a stick and nicely browned before the fire. When my canoemen had time to prepare the bear's feet and boil them they were quite a luxury. In fact, the three great luxuries specially prized by the denizens of that country are, the heaver's tails, the moose's nose, and the bear's paws. Rarely was a deer shot on those canoe trips, unless it happened to be in the far north regions, where occasionally one was caught swimming far out from land in a great lake. When one was thus killed, there was of course abundance of food, but so little of it could be carried with us, that the larger portion had to be left to be devoured by wolves, wolverines, or other wild animals. However, in leaving all this meat on the trail the words of the Psalmist would come to us:

"He giveth to the beast his food, and to the young ravens which cry." Perhaps it was only carrying out His great purposes, when we thus left all this food for some of His creatures to whom, "He giveth their meat in due season."

Wild ducks, geese, and other aquatic birds were occasionally shot, affording us most savoury food as did also the beavers wild-cats, and muskrats.

Our nights were spent where the day's journey ended. Missionaries in nearly all lands can generally find some human, habitation in which to obtain or prepare their food and spend the night. As a child, I used to listen with intense interest to my beloved father, who for many years had been a pioneer missionary in what were then known as the wilds of Upper Canada—tell of his adventures. Many had been his hardships and dangers, but I remember he used to say, that he could generally find the comfortable log-cabin of a friendly settler in which to pass the night. The trail in the wild north land leads through regions of country thousands of miles in extent, where there is not even to be found a leather tepee or a birch-bark wigwam, much less a house. The result was, when making such journeys, we had to do the next best thing, and that was to camp at the spot where night overtook us. Of course we were on the lookout for as comfortable a place as it was possible to find. A smooth dry granite rock for our bed, and dry wood with which to make our fires, where we cooked our food and dried our clothes, were always considered the essential requisites for a comfortable camp. Warm days alternated with damp and chilly ones, but the nights were generally cold. The bright warm camp-fire was always welcomed with great delight after a day's journey of sixty miles on the trail. Pleasant indeed are the memories of happy restful hours so spent, when the good honest day's work was done, and the time of rest well earned. After the hearty evening meal and prayers, it was each a luxury to be able to stretch our cramped limbs before a glorious camp-fire on the rocky shore of some great river or picturesque lake. Then the attempt to read even some favourite author was not always a great success. It seemed more congenial just to lie there, and muse and watch the dying of the day as the brightness gradually faded out of the western sky, and the stars in their modest way, one by one, came out into conscious vision, until the whole heavens were lit up by their radiance. The only sounds were the roar of the distant cataract, the music of the running stream, the rippling of the waves at our feet, broken some nights by the occasional cry of a wild bird or beast, from among the trees of the encircling forest. The quiet, picturesquely garbed men in their statuesque attitudes added much to the attractiveness of the surroundings.

Then at night very close to the heart, and appropriate, were the words of the Psalmist: "The heavens declare the glory of God, and the firmament showeth His handiwork;" and, "When I consider thy heavens the work of thy fingers, the moon and stars which thou hast ordained; what is man that thou art mindful of him, and the son of man that thou visitest him?"

But the nights spent on the Indian trail, were not always so delightful, or so conducive to lofty and celestial sentiments. When the cyclonic winds howled around us through the long night hours, blowing with such fury that it requited all of our watchfulness and strength to prevent canoe, blankets, and bundles from being blown into the lake or river, our thoughts were not among the stars. Sometimes the black thunderclouds gathered and the rain fell upon us in torrents, putting out our fires, perhaps before our evening meal was cooked, drenching us completely, and continuing sometimes so long that we had not a dry stitch upon us for days together. Under such circumstances, while ringing some quarts of water out of our clothes, or from the blankets in which we had slept, there was no disposition to sentimentalise about the rippling of the waves on the shore or the distant waterfall.

Thus in storm as in sunshine, it was necessary that the missionary and his faithful canoemen should be on the trail, if the Book were to be carried, and its glorious truths proclaimed to those wandering people in their wigwam homes, in regions so remote and inaccessible that in no other way could they be reached during the brief summer months. However, in spite of its hardships and dangers, the results accomplished more than compensated for them all. Physical sufferings are not worthy of record, where successful work has been done in the conversion of immortal souls for whom the Saviour died. Many have been the trophies won and marvellous the transformations wrought as the result of these difficult trips on the Indian trail. The missionaries, numbers of whom are still toiling upon them, rejoice that they are counted worthy to endure such hardness, and to be "in perils oft" for His glory, and for the salvation of those for whom He died.

As regards some abiding results attained by these adventurous trips, one or two incidents are here recorded.

On these long journeys, the missionary generally carried with him a small assortment of medicines. He well knew that many a hard heart could be reached, and many a prejudice overcome, by the healing of some afflicted member of the family, when all other means for influencing them for good, had for the time being failed.

At one remote pagan village dwelt a man who had refused most positively to become a Christian. When urged to accept of Christianity he had most emphatically repeated the expression most common among them: "As my fathers lived and died, so will I."

He came to me one day in a state of much perplexity, and after speaking about several things, mentioned the thankfulness that was in his heart on account of my having cured his wife, who had been sick a long time. The way in which he expressed himself, however, showed the great ignorance under which he was living. His words were something like these, and most emphatically were they uttered:

"Missionary, my wife was long sick. I went to the medicine man of my people to cure her. He tried and tried, but he could not do her any good. Then I came to you, and your medicines cured her, and she soon got well. So I believe, that as your medicine is stronger than that of the medicine men of our religion, your religion must be better than ours. My wife and I have talked it over, and we want to sit at your feet, and learn of this new way."

Of course there was a good deal in his mind that was erroneous and I had to explain myself literally and enlighten him, ere I could begin to teach him the truths of the Gospel. However, I had won his heart, and that was half of the battle. Now predisposed toward the truth, he and his wife gladly accepted it. They became sincere and earnest Christians, and were both made a blessing and a benediction to their people.

There was a great hunter who had an only son. He had a number of daughters, but they were as nothing in his sight in comparison with his little boy. One day the child fell sick, and the medicine man of the tribe was sent for in great haste, a famous old conjuror by the name of Tapastanum. He had some knowledge of roots and herbs, but like the other conjurors of his nation, pretended to depend upon his incantations and conjurings to effect his cures. With a great deal of ceremony he brought out his sacred medicine bag, his charms, and rattle and drum. Then arraying himself in the most hideous manner possible, he began his wild incantations. He howled and yelled, he shook his rattle and beat his drum. All however was in vain. The child rapidly became worse as the days passed. Seeing that there was no improvement, the father became thoroughly alarmed and lost all faith in Tapastanum's power. Fearing however to offend him, he gave him some presents of tea and tobacco, and told him that he need not trouble himself to come again. Up to this time he had refused to listen to the missionary's teachings. He had been loud and almost persecuting in his opposition to the preaching of the Gospel among his people, and had refused to come where the friendly Indians gathered under the trees to hear the Word read and explained.

Indian-like however, he had been most observant, and it had not escaped his notice that some cures had been effected by the pale face that had been too difficult for the native medicine men. So, when he saw his little boy getting worse and worse, in spite of all the yells and antics of the conjuror, so soon as he had dismissed him, he came for the missionary, and in a tone very different from that which he had first used, almost begged him to come and save his little boy.

"I will do the best I can," said the missionary, who was thankful for an opportunity thus, perhaps, to win his friendship and to lead him to the cross.

When he examined the boy he found that it was a serious
case of inflammation, so he candidly told the father, that as
the disease had run so long it was hard to say whether he
would be able to cure him or not, but he would gladly do
his best. The Indian father urged him to begin at once to do
all that was possible to save his boy; saying, that he would
be so glad if his child recovered, and would not blame the
missionary if he died.

Prompt remedies were applied, and with God's blessing,
and careful nursing, the child recovered, greatly to the joy
of the father.

Not long after, as the missionary gathered the people
together for religious service, he was pleased to see,
leaning against a distant tree, the once stubborn old Indian
whose son had been healed. It was evident that he was
anxious to hear what that missionary who had cured his boy
had to say, and jet, he was still too proud to come and sit
with the friendly Indians, who were anxious to learn about
the message which the Great Spirit had sent to the people.
So he compromised by taking a position on the outskirts of
the audience.

Fortunately the missionary was gifted with a strong clear
voice, so without any apparent effort, he told the story of
God's love in Jesus Christ in a tone that could be distinctly
heard by all, even by the distant hunter leaning against the
tree.

Very attentively did that Indian listen to all that was said,
and so interested was he, that at the next service he stood at
a tree considerably nearer the speaker. The next service he

was in the midst of the audience, and a few weeks later he was at the Cross, a happy converted man.

It was interesting and delightful to listen to his after apologies, and chidings of himself for his stubborn opposition to that in which he now so delighted. Among other things he would say:

"But missionary, you know that I was so foolish and stubborn. I was then blind and deaf; but now I have rubbed the dust out of my eyes, pulled the moss out of my ears, so now I see clearly and hear all right. Then, I could only say hard things against the Book which I thought was only for the white man, but now, I have found that it is for every one, and I love to think and talk about the good things that it has brought to us."

Long centuries ago Isaiah prophesied:

"Then the eyes of the blind shall be opened, and the ears of the deaf shall be unstopped;

"Then shall the lame man leap as an hart, and the tongue of the dumb sing;

"For in the wilderness shall waters break out, and streams in the desert."

Here in this wild north land, as, thank God, it has been on many other mission fields, this glorious prophecy had been, and is being, most literally fulfilled. Eyes long spiritually blinded are now open to behold the blessed light, deaf ears have been unstopped and now hear His loving voice, and tongues unloosened by His power make the wilderness vocal with His praise.

Chapter Three.

Practical Work in Indian Homes.

Since the opening up of the heart of Africa, by the indomitable courage and zeal of such men as Speke and Moffat, Baker and Livingstone, Stanley and Cameron, Bishop Taylor and others, perhaps one of the least known portions of this habitable globe is the northern part of the great Dominion of Canada. The discovery of the rich gold mines in the great Yukon River district—the greater number by far being in Canadian territory—is attracting attention to that part of the hitherto unknown north-western portion of the great Dominion, and will doubtless lead to its becoming better known.

It is true that there are vast regions of this great country that are of but little value to civilised people as a home. Still there are hundreds of millions of acres, of land as fertile as any in the world, and thousands of people are crowding in every year and taking possession of what will yet become one of the greatest wheat producing portions of the globe.

From east to west, through the Dominion runs the great Canada Pacific Railway, the longest in the world. This great road has not only broken the long silence of the wilderness and opened up the grandest route to the Orient, but it has also unsettled the Indians in their prairie and forest retreat; it has not only brought trade to their wigwam villages but also the missionary with the Bible to their very doors.

But north of these new provinces where the whistle of the iron horse is heard, are vast regions that are as free from the inroads of the adventurous pioneer as is the Desert of Sahara. This is a country of magnificent lakes and rivers with their untold wealth of fish. Its vast forests and morasses abound in fur-bearing animals of great value. Bears and wolves, reindeer and moose, and many other animals which the Indians love to hunt, exist in large numbers.

The Indian tribes of these northern regions live altogether by hunting and fishing. They are not warlike, as are the tribes of the great prairies, but in their pagan state have many vile and abominable practices, which show that they are just as bad as those who delight in war and as much in need of the Gospel.

Missionaries of the different denominations have gone into these remote regions, have lived amidst many privations, and have given their lives to the blessed work of Christianising, and then civilising these long neglected people. They have not toiled in vain. Thousands have renounced their paganism and become earnest, genuine Christians. The missionary life in such a land and among such a people is, as might be well imagined, very different from that in other countries.

As these mission fields are in such high latitudes the winter is very long and severe. Hence, the habitations to be at all comfortable must be very warmly built. There is no limestone in that land, and consequently, no lime. As a poor substitute, mud is used. The houses are built with a framework of squared timber which is well logged up, and the chinks well packed with moss and mud. When this is thoroughly dry, and made as air-tight as possible, the building is clapboarded, and lined with tongued and grooved boards. Double windows are used to help keep out the bitter cold. When well built and cared for, some of these homes are fairly comfortable; very different from the wretched, uncomfortable abodes some of the early missionaries were content to dwell in.

As great forests are everywhere in those regions, wood is used for fuel instead of coal. Great box stoves are kept red hot day and night from October until May.

The food used by the missionaries was the same as that on which the Indians lived. Flour was almost unknown. Fish and game afforded subsistence to nearly all. It is true that, many years ago, the great Saskatchewan, brigades of boats came to Norway house and York factory loaded down with vast quantities of pemmican and dried buffalo meat; but long since the great herds of buffalo have been exterminated, and the far-famed pemmican is now but a memory of the past. The last time I saw the wharves of the Hudson Bay Company's post at Norway House piled up with bags of pemmican, was in 1871. This pemmican was pounded buffalo meat, mixed with the tallow and preserved in large bags made out of the green hides of the slaughtered animals, and was the food that for some months of each year gave variety to our fish diet. It was healthy and nourishing to persons of good appetites and unimpaired digestive organs; but to those not to the "manner born," or unaccustomed to it all their days, it appeared, whether cooked or raw, as partaking more of the nature of soap grease, than of anything more inviting. Cut it has gone to return no more: much to the satisfaction of some, and to the regret of others.

I and my Indian fishermen used to catch about ten thousand white fish in gill nets every October and November. These we hung up on great stages where they froze as solid as stones. A few hundred we would pack away in the snow and ice for use in the following May, when those left on the stages began to suffer from the effects of the spring warmth. These ten thousand fish were needed by the missionary's family and his dogs: the faithful dogs, from whom so much was required, lived on them all the time, while the missionary's family had them on the table twenty-one times a week for six months.

During the winter we had certain varieties of game which I shot, or which the Indian hunters brought in and exchanged with us for tea, sugar, cotton, flannels, or other things. All trade was done by barter, as there was no money then in the land. During the spring and summer months, occasionally, a wild goose or some ducks were obtained, and proved acceptable additions to our bill of fare.

Once or twice during the summer the boats of the Hudson Bay Company—the great trading corporation of the country—brought us from civilisation, our yearly supplies. These consisted of: a few bags of flour, a keg of bolster, a can of coal oil, tea, sugar, soap, and medicines. They also brought an assortment of plain, but good, articles of clothing and dry goods which we required in our own household, and with which we also paid the Indians whom we had to hire, as fishermen, dog-drivers, canoemen or guides on my long journeys over the great mission field which was several hundreds of miles square.

So many were the calls upon us on account of the sickness and terrible poverty of the people, that often our little stock of flour was soon gone. Other luxuries quickly followed, and is the mission home, as in the wigwams of the natives, the great staple was fish, fish, fish.

So many have inquired how Mrs Young and I managed so long to live and thrive, and keep up our health and spirits, on an almost exclusive fish diet, that I will here give the plan we pursued.

We were in good health, and charmed with, and thankful for, our work. We both had so much to do, and were kept very busy either in our own cosy little log house home, or outside among the Indians, that our appetites were generally very good and we were ready for our meals as soon as they were ready for us. Still, after all, the very monotony of the unchangeable fish diet sometimes proved too much for us. We would, perhaps, be seated at the break fast table, neither of us with any appetite for the fish before us. We would sip away at our cups of tea without apparently noticing that the fish were untested, and chat about our plans for the day.

"My dear," I would say, "what are you going to do to-day?"

"I am going to have Kennedy harness up my dogs, and drive me up the river to Playgreen point to see how that old sick woman is getting on and take her the warm blanket I promised her. I will also stop to see how those sick babies are, and how Nancy's little twins are prospering. In the afternoon I want to drive over to York village and see Oosememou's sick wife—What is your day's programme?"

To my good wife's question, my answer would be after this fashion:

"Well, first of all, as word has come that the wolves have been visiting our fish-cache, Martin Papanekis and I have arranged to drive over there with the dogs to see the extent of the damage. We may be detained some hours making the place so strong, that if they visit it again, which is likely, they will be unable to reach the fish. Then we will spend the rest of the day in that vicinity, visiting and praying with the neighbours."

Having taken our tea, we had prayers, and soon after began to carry out the programmes of the day.

For several winters we kept for our varied duties, a number of dogs. Mrs Young and I each had our favourite dog-trains. So widely scattered were the Indians, and for such diverse reasons did they look to us and claim our attention, that our lives were full, not only of solicitude for their welfare, but we were, sometimes for days together kept on the "go," often travelling many miles each day in visiting the sick and afflicted, and in looking after the interests of those who needed our personal help.

On that particular day in which the conversation above recorded was held, it was after dark ere our work was accomplished and we met in our little dining-room for our evening meal. It was really the first meal of the day; for we had a tacit understanding that when these times arrived that we could not really enjoy our fish diet, we would resolutely put in the whole days work without tasting food. The result was, that when we drew up to the table after having refused the morning breakfast, and ignored the midday meal, we found that our appetite, even for fish, had returned, and we enjoyed them greatly. And what was more, the appetite for them remained with us for some considerable time thereafter.

Hunger is still a good sauce; and we found—and others also have made the same discovery—that when the appetite fails and there is a tendency to criticise, or find fault with the food, or even with the cook, a voluntary abstinence for two or three meals will be most beneficial for mind and body, and bring back a very decided appreciation of some of God's good gifts which hitherto had been little esteemed.

Of course the great and prominent work was the preaching of the Gospel and the teaching of the people to read the Word of God. To this latter work we devote a full chapter and so need not refer to it here. Next perhaps to the direct results obtained by the preaching of the Word, we accomplished the most good by the medical work.

Indians are fond of medicine and are believers in large doses. The hotter the dose is with cayenne pepper, or the more bitter with any powerful drug, the more it is relished, and the greater faith they have in its power to effect a cure. Various were the expedients of some of them to induce us to give them a good strong cup of tea, made doubly hot with red pepper. In their estimation such a dose was good for almost any disease with which they could be afflicted, and was especially welcomed in the cold and wintry days, when the mercury was frozen hard, and the spirit thermometer indicated anything between forty and sixty degrees below zero.

Practical sympathy never failed to reach some hearts, and so influenced them, that they were ultimately brought to Christ.

So poverty stricken were the people, that the opportunities of helping them were many. Looked at from our standpoint of comfort, they had very little with which to make themselves happy. Few indeed were their possessions. Owning the land in common, there was in it no wealth to any one of them; but neither were there any landlords, or rents. All their other possessions were their wigwams, traps, nets, guns, canoes, dogs, and clothing. They lived from hand to mouth, as they had no facilities for keeping any surplus food even if they were ever fortunate enough to secure more than they needed for their immediate wants. If some were successful in killing a number of deer or bears, they made but little attempt at trying to dry or preserve some of the meat for future use. Very rarely, a little deer-pemmican would be made out of some of the venison; but this was an exceptional case. The general plan, was to keep open house after a successful hunt, with the pot boiling continually, everybody welcomed and told to eat heartily while the supply lasted. He was considered a mean man indeed, who, being fortunate in killing a large quantity of game, did not share it with all who happened to come along. This hospitality was often earned to such an extent, that there would be but very little left for the hunter himself, or for his own family.

Thus, life among the Indians for long generations, was a kind of communism. No unfortunate one actually starved to death in the village so long as there was a whitefish or a haunch of venison in the community. It was feast together when plenty comes; starve together when plenty goes. They could not at first understand why, when the missionary had anything in his mission house, he hesitated about giving it out to any one who said he was hungry. This plan, of once a year getting in front the outside world supplies to last a whole year, was indeed a mystery to them. They had an idea that it was very nice to see so many things coming in by the company's boats; but when they were once in the house, the pagan Indians thought that they should be used up as quickly as anybody asked for them. The practice of rationing out the supplies to last for twelve months, was a style of procedure that more than once exposed a missionary, who rigidly adhered to it, to be thought mean, stingy, and very unfriendly. They even questioned the truthfulness of one frugal, careful missionary, who carried out this system. When asked to help some hungry Indians, he refused on the plea that he had nothing left, knowing that that month's supply was gone. They reasoned from the fact, that, they knew that he had the balance of his year's supply stored away.

One very interesting phase of our work, was to help the Indian families, who had moved from a wigwam into a cosy little house, into the mysteries of civilised housekeeping. It is true that these houses were not very large or imposing. They were generally built only of logs, well chinked up with moss and mud, and consisted of but one room, with the fireplace in the end or side. As the people were able, they put up partitions and added various little conveniences. At first, when a family moved into one of these homes, some of its members would be very much inclined to keep to their wigwam habits. As these were very shiftless, and far below what we considered to be their possibilities of methodical and tidy housekeeping, some practical lessons had to be given. As they were willing to learn, various plans and methods were adopted to help them. The following was the most successful and perhaps on the whole, to all concerned, the most interesting. When we were aware that some new houses had been erected and taken possession of by families who had known no other habitations than their wigwams, I would announce from the pulpit on Sabbath, that during the week, in connection with my pastoral visitations, Mrs Young and I would dine at

Pugamagon's house on Monday, on Tuesday with
Oostasemou, and on Wednesday with Oosememou. These
announcements at first caused great consternation among
the families mentioned. When the services were over and
we were leaving the church, we would be accosted by the
men whose names I had mentioned, generally in words like
these:

"Could we believe our ears to-day, when we thought we
heard you say, that you and Ookemasquao, (Mrs Young's
Indian name) were coming over to dine with us?"

"Certainly, your ears are all right. That is what they heard,
and that is what we are thinking of doing," would be our
answer.

"Nothing but fish, have we to set before you," would
generally be their reply, uttered in tones of regret.

"Well, that is all right. It is what we generally eat at home,"
we would reply.

"Well, but we have no table as yet, or chairs, or dishes fit
for you," would be their next objection.

"That is all right, we are coming."

Meantime, their half frightened wives would be seen
standing behind their husbands, most attentively listening
to the conversation.

When they found that this enumeration of the lack of
variety of food and the poverty of their new homes, could
not deter us from our determination to dine with them,
almost in desperation they would say:

"Well, what are we to do to be ready to receive you?"

"That is the very question we wanted you to ask," I would reply. "Now I will tell you what is in our hearts. Have plenty of your fish ready and we will look after the rest of the dinner. But there are several other things about which we are anxious, and to which we want you to attend: first, we want to see when we visit you, how very clean and sweet your new house will be; then, we are also anxious to see, how neat and tidy the members of the family will be; we also wish to see, how bright and polished all your kettles, pots, and plates, will be. We are both coming to your homes as I announced, so be on the lookout and ready for us. I believe we will all have a good time."

Somewhat relieved by this interview, they would start off to their homes.

Soon after breakfast on Monday morning, Mrs Young would have her own dog-train and cariole brought up to the door, aid aided by willing hands, the cariole would be quickly loaded up for the visit to the Indian home announced for that day's visit.

Perhaps it is but right here to state, that we never inflicted these visits upon our Indians except when we had abundance of supplies of some kind or other in the mission house, and were thus able to carry over sufficient, with the fish the family supplied, for a hearty meal. So, in her cariole Mrs Young had, not only this liberal supply of food, with plenty of tea and sugar, but a large tablecloth, dishes, knives, forks, spoons, and other essentials. About nine o'clock she was driven over to the home, where, with a certain amount of trepidation, the expectant family were awaiting her coming. They had been at work very early and never did a floor made of well-planed spruce boards shine whiter. For hours it had been scrubbed; an unlimited amount of elbow-grease aided by some soft soap made out of strong lye and the grease of a fat dog, had done the work most completely. The faces of the children showed that they had been most thoroughly polished, while all the family were arrayed in their Sunday apparel. Every kettle and pot bore evidence of the early hour at which the family had arisen and begun operations.

The instructions given to me, were, that I was not to put in an appearance until about half-past twelve, and I was so interested that I was generally on time.

It was a very gratifying sight that met me, and a very cordial welcome that I received. Every member of the family was simply radiant with happiness and my good wife had most thoroughly caught the contagion of the hour. I, of course, shook hands all round and kissed the fat little baby in its quaint, moss-bag cradle. Then, we were speedily informed of what was very evident, that dinner was ready. There was not a chair or table in the house. The snow white tablecloth was spread out on the almost equally snow white floor, and upon it were placed in order plates, cups, and saucers, knives and forks. Then the dinner which had been cooked in various pots, and pans, at the capacious fireplace, was served up, or rather, down, and in our assigned places we seated ourselves Indian-like, upon the floor. After heaven's blessing was asked, the feast began. The menu was not very elaborate. Spoiled children of luxury, with lost appetites, might have sneered at it, but to us in that land, and especially to this happy Indian family, it was one of the great events of their lives. The missionary and his wife were happy because they saw these poor people so happy.

For perhaps three hours, Mrs Young, had been the
instructor of that Indian motherland her daughters, as under
her direction they prepared that dinner, and they were very
proud of their teacher.

The dinner was pronounced a great success, and after it
was over, and all had had an abundance, the Bible in the
syllabic characters, was brought out and read, when all
devoutly kneeling, the missionary with a glad heart offered
up an earnest prayer for heaven's blessing ever to abide
upon that home.

After prayers I was expected to leave, while Mrs Young
remained for the rest of the day. When she returned to our
mission home in the evening, tired, but very happy over her
day's work, she would give me some glimpses into the
doings of the afternoon. Of course, the first thing, was to
teach the women how, nicely and carefully, to wash and put
away the dishes; then, the house was once more swept up,
when they were ready for the afternoons work. Sometimes
the happy Indian mother was able to bring out a nice piece
of dress cloth, which her now kind. Christian husband, had
bought for her in exchange for his valuable furs. This dress
piece had to be cut and fitted by Mrs Young. When asked
as to how she wished to have it made she would generally
say:

"Please, Ookemasquao, cut it out so that it will be like the
one you had on in church, last Sunday."

So, as far as possible, the dress was cut and fitted in that
style, the sewing of it commenced, and full instructions
given so that the owner might go on working, until she
became perplexed with its intricacies, when she would

come to the mission house for help, and so on until the work was completed.

In addition to thus helping in dressmaking there were lessons to be given in patching and darning, and in lengthening out, or adding to, the dresses of the rapidly growing Indian girls.

Thus, from house to house we went, and for long years after the good results of those visits remained; thus, was a noble ambition stirred in those Indian women's lives to try and keep house like Ookemasquao; and thus, they endeavoured to let their husbands and children see, that no longer did they wish to live in the careless way of the old pagan life, but, as now they had become Christians in their profession, so in their homes, they would have the neatness and cleanliness, that should belong to those who are thus called.

Chapter Four.

How the Gospel is carried: by Canoe in Summer; by Dog-Train in Winter.

That great northern country is a land of innumerable lakes and rivers. Unfortunately, many of the streams abound with rapids, and navigation on them, as generally understood, is an impossibility. Hence, the only way of travelling on them in summer, is in the light birch canoe or in some other craft, so portable, that it can be carried or dragged across the many portages that are so numerous in that land of cataracts and falls.

From time immemorial, the birch canoe has been considered a part of the craft of the Indian. Centuries of its use has enabled him so to perfect it, that although attempts have been made by the white man to improve it, they have not been very successful.

One of our missionaries, who was one of the best canoemen in the country, was conceited enough to imagine, that the beautiful cedar canoe of the white man was superior to the birch-bark ones of the natives. So certain was he of this, that at a good deal of trouble and expense, he had one of the very best models sent to him all the way from Ontario to Norway House. On the beautiful Playgreen lake and other similar places, he enjoyed it amazingly; but when he started off on his missionary touring, the Indians, who are the best judges of these things urged him not to attempt in that beautiful, but unreliable boat, to run the wild rapids of the mighty Nelson or other great rivers. He, however, only laughed at their fears and protestations. A number of them set off together on a long missionary journey, one of the objects of which was, to assist in the building of a new church. For a time, the erection of the little sanctuary in the wilderness went on uninterruptedly, much to the delight of the resident Christian Indians, who had long wished for one in which to worship God.

The securing of sufficient food for the builders, was one of the duties that devolved upon, and gave considerable anxiety to, the missionary. When the supplies which had been secured were about exhausted, and it seemed as though the work of building would have to cease on account of the lack of food, word came through some passing hunters that they had seen abundance of sturgeon sporting at the foot of some great rapids of the Nelson River. As they are considered delicious and nourishing food, an expedition was at once prepared to go and capture as many of them as possible. The missionary himself, an energetic, active man, took charge of the party, and insisted, on going in his beautiful cedar canoe. When they reached the head of the rapids, at the foot of which the sturgeon were reported to have been seen in such numbers, there was a brief rest ere the run down was attempted. The Indians all protested against the missionary's resolve to run such wild rapids in a canoe which they were certain was so unfitted for such a dangerous trip. The missionary, however, was stubborn and unmoved by their entreaties. When they saw that their words availed not, to change his resolve, an old experienced guide said:

"Well, then let one of us go with you, to sit in the stern of your boat and help you to steer, and also, by our weight, to keep the head of your canoe high up as we run the rapids."

This kindly offer to risk and to share the dangers, he also refused, saying, "that he could go in his white man's canoe anywhere an Indian could go in a birch-bark." Their objection to his canoe, was, that it was not built high enough in front, and so when he made the last wild rush in the rapids where the pitch in the waters was so steep, instead of the boat rising like a duck on the mad billows at the foot, it would plunge under like a log and disappear.

Well would it have been for the wilful missionary if he had listened to the advice of these experienced men who knew what they were talking about. He, however, cut them short by ordering them to enter their canoes and go on, and he would soon follow. With regret they left him there, sitting on a rock, leisurely watching them as they began the hazardous trip. With care and skill, the Indians all succeeded in successfully running those dangerous rapids which are as wild and fierce as any in the Saint Lawrence. As quickly as possible they went ashore at the foot, and, with their hearts full of foreboding, clustered at a point where they could watch the missionary make the run.

Alas! their fears were too well grounded. Down the rushing, roaring river, they saw the brave, but rash man, coming. With consummate skill in the upper rapids, did he manage his beautifully polished craft; but when the last wild plunge at the foot was made, both canoe and missionary suddenly disappeared. It was many days ere the poor putrid body was recovered, far away down the great river.

A solitary grave is there on the bank, and a little tombstone set up by loving hands, records the name of this brave, but rash man.

For the manufacture of a first class Indian canoe, the birch-bark must be taken from the tree at the right time of the year with the greatest care. The framework must be arranged with a skill and accuracy that comes only of long practice. The fact is, the first-class canoe-makers, were about as rare among the tribes, as are first-class poets in civilisation. Many Indians could make canoes; but there were a few men whose fame for their splendid crafts, were known far and wide, and who were always able to obtain the highest price for all they could make.

It is really wonderful, considering the cranky nature of a canoe at its best, what journeys can be made in them. My skilled canoeman and I used to run wild rapids, and cross over storm swept lakes of large dimensions. We lived on the game we could shoot as we hurried along, slept on the rocks or sandy beach where night overtook us, and were always thankful when we found the little companies of Indians for whom we were seeking. As they were generally eager to hear the truth, but little time was lost between the religious services. Long sermons and addresses were the order of the day; and often from early morn until late at night, there was only the short intermissions for our hasty meals of fish or game.

As we journeyed on from place to place, our meals were cooked and eaten in the open air, and for days we met no human beings. Our bed was on some balsam boughs, if obtainable; if not, a smooth granite rock or sandy beach did very well. So healthful were we, and so congenial was the work and its surroundings, that there were no sleepless nights, except when sometimes myriads of mosquitoes assailed us, or a fierce thunderstorm swept over us. Then the nights were not so pleasant, and we welcomed the coming of the day, even if, because of the storm, it revealed a damp condition of affairs among our supplies.

This was the general plan of our proceedings: when we reached one of the little Indian villages at a time which had been, perhaps, arranged six months or a year before. All who possibly could come in from contiguous fishing or hunting grounds, were there to meet me; then, for several days services would be held, after which the Indians would return to their different hunting grounds, while I would again launch my canoe and with my skilled paddlers, push on to some other point, where would be gathered another company of Indians awaiting my arrival and longing to hear the glorious Gospel of the Son of God.

Very precious was the Word to those people so isolated. The coming of the missionary in his canoe to preach to them, and perhaps teach them how to read for themselves the precious Book, was one of the few happy breaks during the brief summer months in their lonely, monotonous lives. They were ever on the lookout for my coming, and especially did those who had renounced their paganism and accepted Christianity give me a hearty welcome, even if it was expressed in their quiet, dignified way.

The Indian's alertness and keenness of hearing, as well as of seeing, was something remarkable to me. The following is a good illustration of it. One summer, when thus travelling, I was on the lookout for some friendly Indians whose camping place was determined each summer by the abundance of the food supply. Anxious to make as much of the time as possible, my men and I were paddling away in our canoe at four o'clock in the morning. To hasten our progress, we pushed out into the centre of the great river, down which we were travelling, as there the current was much more rapid than near the shore. At that early hour, the morning mists still lay low and dense on either side, completely hiding from view every object on the shore.

While thus pushing on between those walls of vapoury
mist, we were startled by the rapid firing of guns. To me
this was a decided mystery, but it was at once understood
by my experienced canoemen. Quickly turning the head of
our canoe in the direction from which came the tiring, they
paddled through the now rapidly disappearing vapours, and
there on the shore we descried a company of friendly
Indians on the lookout for our coming. Their ears had been
of more service than their eyes; for although they had been
unable to see us, their practiced ears had caught the sound
of our paddles. After greeting us most cordially, they
produced some smoked reindeer tongues and other native
delicacies which they had brought for the missionary. Some
very suggestive and profitable religious services were
enjoyed there by the riverside. For the comfort and
encouragement of those who had already become His
children we talked of the loving kindnesses and
providential care of our Heavenly Father. We also pleaded
with those who had not yet decided to renounce the
paganism of their forefathers, to do so speedily and to
accept of the religion of the Lord Jesus Christ.

Thus the work went on, and through many happy summers,
my canoe was afloat for days on many waters, while as a
glad messenger, I travelled through the wilderness
beseeching men and women to be reconciled to God.

Of the dog-travelling in that land so much has been written,
that but a short account need here be given. Winter begins
in those regions in the latter part of October and continues
without any perceptible break until April. So immense,
however, are the ice-fields on the great lakes, that they do
not all disappear until a month or six weeks later. One
winter I was able to make quite a long journey with my
dog-trains, arriving home as late as the eighteenth of May.

At that date, however, the snow had all disappeared and the frost was nearly all out of the ground.

The cold is intense, the spirit thermometer indicating from thirty to sixty below zero. We have seen the mercury frozen as solid as lead for weeks together. For months milk is frozen into cakes like marble. We used to carry large pieces of it wrapped up in a newspaper, and when at the camp-fire we desired a little in our cup of tea, we cut it off with an axe. As will be seen from this we had about seven months of bright cold winter. During all that time there was not a thaw, the snow was never soft, and there was no dampness in the air or under foot. Soft deer skin moccasins are very much superior to civilised boots or shoes under such conditions.

There are no roads in that vast country. The frost King freezes up every lake and stream, and hardens into adamant every muskeg and quaking bog. The snow covers everything with its great mantle of beauty, and makes it possible to travel on snow-shoes or by dog-train through vast regions absolutely impassable in the summer months. Horses or other large animals, are absolutely worthless for travel in such regions. The snow is a great leveller. It fills up many a dangerous pitfall and puts such a cushion on the logs and rocks, that upsets or falls are only laughed at by the dog-travellers as they merrily dash along. The only drawbacks to a tumble down a steep declivity of some hundreds of feet, as once befell the writer, were the laughter of his comrades, and the delay incident to digging him out of the snowdrift at the bottom, which was anywhere from twenty to thirty feet deep. These accidents and delays were not frequent; and, although there were hardships and sufferings, there were many things to instruct and interest, and to break the monotony of winter travelling in that lonely land.

In the coldest, brightest, sunniest days, the fitful mirage played its strange antics with distant landscapes, and at times brought within near vision places many miles away. Sometimes circle within circle appeared around the sun, until as many as four were distinctly visible; each circle at times having within it four mock suns—sixteen mock suns visible at the same time was a sight worth going a long distance to see. Strange to say, the Indians dreaded the sight of them, as they declared they were always the forerunners of blizzard storms; and the more vivid these sun-dogs, as they called them, the more dreadful would be the storm.

But the most fascinating and glorious of all the celestial phenomena of those glorious regions, are the Northern Lights—the Aurora Borealis. Confined to no particular months of the year, we have seen them flashing and quivering through the few hours of the short nights following the hottest days in July or August, as well as in the long cold nights of the winter months. They would sometimes linger on all night in their weird beauty, until lost in the splendour of the coming day. A description of them has often been attempted by writers of northern scenes, and I have to confess, that I have been rash enough to try it elsewhere; but their full glories are still unwritten and perhaps ever will be. They appear to belong to the spiritual rather than to the earthly; and there are times when they so dazzle and overwhelm, that it does seem as though only the language of spirits is adequate to the task of describing them. Then they are so changeable. Never have I seen two great exhibitions of them alike. At first they are of purest white; but when the scintillations begin, they take on

every colour of the rainbow. Sometimes they appear in
great brilliant arcs, as in the illustration. At other times they
are simply ribbons of wavy undulations that seem to
soothe, as well as charm, with their rhythmic motions and
ever changing hues. At still other times they are mighty
armies of disciplined warriors going out to conflict. Then,
when they seem wearied with their warlike deeds, they
appear to marshal all their forces; and, fairly filling the
northern heavens, to rush on, and up, until the very zenith
is reached, where they form a corona of such dazzling
splendour, that it really seems as though the longing prayer
of the church militant was being fulfilled; and, that
universal triumph had come to the world's Redeemer here,
and now the angelic and redeemed hosts of heaven and
earth are bringing forth the Royal Diadem to "crown Him
Lord of all."

The dogs which we use in the dog-trains, are generally of
any breed that has in it size, endurance, and sagacity. The
Esquimaux breed of dogs formerly predominated; but in
later years there has been such an admixture of other
varieties, that a pure Esquimaux dog is now a rarity except
at some of the most northern posts and missions. My
worthy predecessor among the Crees, left me a train of
mongrels, that were good enough for hauling wood and fish
for the mission; and also for the short trips to the places
near home where I held weekly services; but when I
attempted to make the long journeys of hundreds of miles
to the remote parts of my great mission field, which was
larger than all England or the state of New York, they
proved miserable failures. Travelling with such dogs, was
like the experience of the man who, in the olden times, paid
first-class fare to ride in a packet boat on the Erie canal,
from New York to Buffalo, and then drove a horse on the
towpath all the way. So, after nearly killing myself

travelling with weak or lazy dogs, having to walk or run on snowshoes all the time on account of their inability to draw me, I resolved, if possible, to become the owner of better ones. I appealed to some good friends in civilisation to aid me, and the result was, that I was soon supplied with some of the finest dogs that could be obtained. Among them, Jack and Cuffy, the gifts of Senator Sanford of Hamilton, were never equalled. Through the kindness of James Ferrier, Esquire, of Montreal, five beautiful Saint Bernards were obtained from Mrs Andrew Allan. Dr Mark of Ottawa, and other friends also remembered me, with the result, that soon I had some of the finest dog-trains in the land. These civilised dogs had all the good qualities of the Esquimaux without any of their thievish tricks. They proved themselves equal in their endurance and sagacity; and only lacked in that their feet seemed more easily to become injured and sore.

The dog-sleds are ten feet long and eighteen inches wide. They are used to carry our bedding and supplies, as often for days and nights together we are entirely dependent on our loads for food and lodgings. These miscellaneous loads are well packed up in the great deer skin wrappers and so securely tied to the sleds, that no matter how many may be the upsets, the loads never become disarranged. My own sled, which was called a "cariole," was one of the usual oak sleds with parchment sides and a firm back attached. Sometimes these carioles were handsomely painted and were very comfortable vehicles in which to ride. When well wrapped up in fur robes, with plenty of fat meat to eat, splendid dogs to draw you, and loving loyal Indian attendants with you dog-travelling was not without its pleasures and enjoyments; especially if the sun was bright, the icy pavement under you free from drifting snows, and the temperature not colder than forty degrees below zero. It was a different thing, however, when blizzards howled around you and the air was so fall of the fine cutting particles of icy snow, that it was dangerous to expose any part of the face to their pitiless attacks. Then it was, that the marvellous skill of the experienced Indian-guide was seen, and we were led on amidst such miserable surroundings with an accuracy and speed that seemed almost incredible.

The camp, when the day's travel was ended—especially if blizzards had assailed us—was a welcomed spot, even if it was only a whole day out in the snow on the sheltered side on some dense spruce or balsam grove. At times we were able to find places in which thus to camp that were quite picturesque. When the halt for the night was called by the guide, the first thing done was to unharness our faithful dogs. Our snow-shoes were improvised as shovels, and from the spot selected as our resting place, the snow was quickly piled up in a great bank at our rear; and, sometimes, if the night threatened to be unusually severe, on each side of us.

Then the great roaring fire of dry wood, at which we cooked our suppers, thawed out the fish for our dogs, and warmed our half frozen bodies, was very welcome. When supper was eaten, and prayers, so sweet and profitable to us all, were over, how delightful to sit down on our robes and spend some hours in pleasant chat ere my bed was made and I was cosily and thoroughly tucked in by my faithful comrades. It was hard at first to sleep with the head completely covered; there was such a sense of smothering, that I often ran the risk of the freezing rather than the smothering. One night, perhaps because of this suffocating sensation, I unconsciously uncovered my head. After a time I awoke suddenly to consciousness, to find that I was trying to pull off my now frozen nose which I thought was the end of an axe handle.

We fed our dogs on fish, giving them only one meal a day, and that one, when the day's work was done. To feed them in the morning, caused them to be sluggish and stupid for some time thereafter; and the same happened if they were fed at noon. Long experience has shown, that the dogs thrive the best, and are able to do the most work, on one good meal given to them before their long night's rest. The dog-shoes, which are so essential to their comfort and recovery when a foot is frozen or badly injured, are much prized by them. These shoes are made out of a warm English cloth called duffle, and are in shape like a large mit without a thumb. An old dog that has once become accustomed to dog shoes, is ever hankering after them when on a long cold trip. Sometimes, they will come and most comically hold up their feet to be shod. At other times, they have been known to come into camp and there lie down on their backs, and, holding up their four feet, plead most ludicrously and importunately for these warm woollen shoes. Some of them get very cunning at their work, and shirk from doing their share of the pulling; and yet, to avoid discovery, will appear to be doing more work than any other dog in the train.

But this dog travelling was hard work at best; and dogs, as well as their master, were always glad when the long journeys were ended and a welcome rest for a little while could be taken, to heal up the wounds and frost bites, and gather strength for the next trip.

Good was accomplished, and that was the great reward for all the risks run and sufferings endured. Many for whom Christ died, would never up to the present hour, have heard the Gospel or have seen the Book, if it had not been for the missionary carrying it to them by the canoe in summer, and the dog-train in winter. Thank God, many of them have heard and have accepted gladly the great salvation thus brought to them. With its reception into their hearts and lives, marvellous have been the transformations. Where the devil-dance, and ghost-dance, and other abominations, performed to the accompaniment of the conjurer's rattle or the monotonous drumming of the medicine man, once prevailed and held the people in a degrading superstition, the house of prayer has now been erected, and the wilderness has become vocal with the sweet songs of Zion. Lives once impure and sinful have been transformed by the Gospel's power, and a civilisation real and abiding, has come in to bless and to add to their comfort for this life, while they dwell in a sweet and blessed assurance of life eternal in the world to come.

Chapter Five.

God on the Rock, or how the Indians are taught to read the Book.

The British and Foreign Bible Society, the American Bible Society, and other kindred institutions that print and scatter the Word of God, have been, and are, of incalculable benefit to the missionaries.

Long ago the Psalmist said: "The entrance of thy words giveth light;" and blessedly and gloriously is this truth being realised.

No matter where a missionary goes, he feels much hampered if he has not the Book in the language of the people. It is a matter of thankfulness, that in these later years—thanks to these glorious Bible Societies—there is hardly a land or nation where a missionary can go, but he will find the Bible printed in the language or languages of that nation, and offered to the people at rates so reasonable, that the poorest of the poor may have it if they will. But it was not always so, and we need not go back to Wickliffe or Tyndal to read of difficulties in the way of presenting to the common people the Word of God in their own tongue. All the great missionary societies in their earlier days had their Careys, and Morrisons, and Duffs, who struggled on, and persevered against oppositions and difficulties that to ordinary mortals would have been insurmountable, and would have filled them with despair.

The difficulties that John Eliot had to overcome ere he was able to give the Bible to the Indians of New England, were numerous and exasperating; but his indomitable will carried him through to ultimate success. Sad indeed is it to think, that there is not a man, woman or child of them left to read his Bible. All the tribes for whom, at such a cost of tears and difficulties, he translated the Book, are gone. The greed for land and the cruelties of the early settlers, were too much for the poor Indian. From his different reservations where Eliot, Brainard, Mayhews, and other devoted friends tried to save him, he was driven back, back, with such destruction and loss at each move, that ultimately he was simply wiped out. And so to-day, in the library of Harvard University and in a very few other places, there are to be found copies of Eliot's Bible; sealed books, which no man can read; a sad evidence of "Man's inhumanity to man."

One of the most signal triumphs in giving the Bible to a people in their own language, and printed in a way so simple as to be very easily acquired by them, is that of the translation and printing of the Book in the syllable characters. These syllabic characters were invented by the Rev. James Evans, one of the early Methodist missionaries to the scattered tribes of Indians in what were then known as the Hudson Bay Territories. For some years Mr Evans had been employed as a missionary among the Indians who resided on different reservations in the Province of Ontario, then known as Upper Canada. At the request of the parent Wesleyan Missionary Society, and at the solicitation of the Hudson Bay Fur-trading Company, Mr Evans, accompanied by some devoted brother missionaries went into those remote northern regions to begin missionary operations. Mr Evans and some of his companions travelled all the way from Montreal to Norway House, on the Nelson River, in a birch-bark canoe. A look at the map will give some idea of the length and hardships of such a journey in those days. But they succeeded in accomplishing it; and with glad hearts began their blessed work of the evangelisation of the natives.

Missionary methods must necessarily differ in different lands. The missionary to succeed must be a man who can adopt himself to his surroundings; and he must be quick to see where success can be most easily attained. Here was a people who were fishermen and hunters, living far north of the agricultural regions. As hunters, they were ever on the go, so that it was almost an impossibility to keep them long enough in one place to teach them to read in the ordinary way. Over these difficulties Mr Evans pondered and worked and, after any amount of experimenting and failure, succeeded in inventing and perfecting that is known as the syllabic characters.

These very simple characters each represent a syllable, so all the difficulties of learning to spell are done away with. In prosecuting his work, Mr Evans had to labour under many disadvantages. Living in a land so remote from civilisation, he had but little material on which to experiment, and but few facilities to aid him. From the fur-traders he begged a few sheets of the lead that lines the interior of tea chests. This he melted into suitable pieces, out of which he carved his first type. For paper he was obliged at first to use birch bark. His ink was manufactured out of the soot from his chimney and sturgeon oil. Yet with these rude appliances he succeeded in being able to print portions of the Scriptures and some hymns in the language of the Cree Indians. When the story of his marvellous invention reached England, generous friends came to his assistance. From some of his types, as models, a generous supply was cast; these, with a good hand printing press and all necessary supplies of paper, ink, and other essentials, were shipped to him by the Hudson Bay Company, to

Norway House. For years the work of printing portions of the Word of God was there prosecuted, until at length the British and Foreign Bible Society took up the work, and now, all the Bibles the people require are most cheerfully furnished them by that most generous and glorious society.

The love of the Christian Indians for their Bible is very gratifying. So great a comfort and solace is it to them in their solitary wigwams and lonely hunting-camps, that nothing will induce them to leave it out of their pack. The trail may be rough and the journey of many days duration; food may have to be carried on their backs for days together so that every pound of weight has to be determined upon; days of hunger must be faced ere the journey ends and abundance of game is reached, yet the Great Book is ever carried as the most prized of all their possessions. Such a thing as a Christian Indian throwing out his Bible, when in an emergency his load had to be lightened, I have never known. Their work as hunters gives them a good deal of leisure time, which enables them to be diligent students of the Book. When in the beginning of the winter, they go to the distant hunting grounds, the hunting lodge is erected, and the traps and snares and other appliances for capturing the game are all arranged. Then, especially in the capture of some kinds of game, they have to allow some days to pass ere they visit the traps. This is to allow all evidences of their presence to disappear, as some of the most valuable fur-bearing animals have a wonderful power of detecting the presence of man, and will not approach either his traps or trail, until some considerable time after the hunter had finished his work and retired. During these long waitings in their wigwams, or hunting lodges, the Indians have not much with which to interest themselves; the result is, the Bible has come to them as a wonderful benediction. Its startling incidents and stories, become more prized than the legends and myths that have come down to them from their forefathers, and have been repeated over and over in their hearing by the old story-tellers of the tribe. Then, when the revelation of God's love in the gift of His Son has been proclaimed to, and received by them—and here in this Book they can read it for themselves—they are filled with grateful and adoring love, and the Book is indeed most precious.

As I journeyed among these wonderful people, I carried as part of my outfit, a number of these syllabic Bibles, and no gift was more acceptable to those who had but lately renounced their paganism and given their hearts to God. In some way or other they had acquired a knowledge of the syllables, so that the acquisition of a Bible that they could call their own, was a treasure most prized and used. Amongst those, who until my visit had never seen a Bible or heard a missionary, there were conflicting ideas regarding the Book. Some, at first, were afraid of it. It was "great medicine," and only for the white man. One old conjurer who boasted of his supernatural powers and of the wonderful things he could do by the aid of his "medicines," failing signally when I challenged him to show his power, declared, that it was because of the Book which I carried in my pocket. Then, I permitted an Indian to take the Book some distance away; and when he still failed, he protested that it was because I had so much of it in my head or heart. Of course this feeling of fear for the Book quickly left them as they became acquainted with it. When Christianity is accepted, there comes a great love for the precious volume that has in it so much information of things about which they are in such ignorance, and that reveals the love of the Great Spirit for His Indian children.

The missionaries employed simple and primitive ways to teach the syllabic characters to those who knew them not, but who were anxious to learn. Sometimes with a lead pencil on a piece of board or birch-bark, the characters were drawn and slowly and carefully gone over, time and time again, until they were completely mastered. When pencils gave out, the end of a burnt stick, or a piece of coal from the fire, had to serve as a substitute.

Our illustration will show one of my methods used at Burntwood River far up in the Nelson River country. I had the honour of being the first missionary who ever reached the Indians of that section and preached to them the Gospel. They are a fine company of Indians, and I found, that with the few exceptions of some old conjurers and medicine men and polygamists, the people were not only glad to see me, but anxious to hear and accept the Gospel of our Lord Jesus Christ. I visited them twice a year and began the work; but to my beloved first colleague, the Rev. John Semmens, was given the work of establishing the mission. On my visits, which as usual were made with my dogs in winter and by canoe in summer, I had to gather the Indians for religious services as best I could. The large kitchen of the Hudson Bay Company's trading post was put at my disposal by the officer in charge, who was ever kindly disposed toward the good work. In this, as well as in the poor wigwams of the natives, we met, and sang, and prayed, and explained to them as well as possible the plan of salvation—God's great love toward them.

In the short brilliant summer the work was very much more pleasant. Then, under the beautiful trees, or where the great rocks rose up around us and cast their welcome shadows, we could gather the people and talk of the loving Heavenly

Father; not only of His Creative power, but of His
redeeming love in the gift of His beloved Son.

In my missionary experiences I have found, that the
majority of men are sick of sin. Down in the human heart
there is a longing for something which is only really
satisfied by the acceptance of the Lord Jesus Christ. It is
true that these inner feelings may be long hidden from
outer vision, or there may be an endeavour to satisfy their
cravings by the vigorous exercise of all the religious
ceremonies that have been revealed to them in their
idolatrous or pagan surroundings; but when they can be
induced to speak out and unburden their very souls, their
bitter wailing cry is one of dissatisfaction and unrest.
Happy is the missionary who can so win the confidence of
a people thus dissatisfied, that they will reveal to him their
heart's burdens and longings. His victory is more than half
assured. Christ in His fulness, lovingly presented to such,
and accepted by them, is soon in their hearts a satisfying
portion.

The missionary ever finds among all classes of pagan
people that the Book is always considered a mysterious and
wonderful volume. Its marvellous incidents ever attract.
They never tire of the services where it has a prominent
place. Sermons, even though hours in duration, if full of its
truths, will be attentively listened to.

One day at one of these places where I was holding some
extended services, I said to the friendly Indians who were
around me: "Would you not like to read this Book for
yourselves?" A chorus of hearty affirmative answers, was
the quick response. It did not take us long to organise our
school, for it was indeed a primitive affair. I was fortunate
in having a goodly number of syllabic Bibles, which, at a

great deal of trouble, we had brought with us in our canoe. We had carried them across many a portage and had guarded them from injury in many a storm. Not one person in that audience except my boatmen, knew a letter or syllabic character. We had no primary books, which are considered so essential in organising a school that has to begin at first principles; we had not even a slate, pencil, paper, or blackboard. However, "necessity is the mother of invention," and it was so here.

Near at hand was a huge rock that towered up like a house, one side of it being as smooth as a wall. This constituted an admirable substitute for a blackboard. Burnt sticks from the camp-fire, where our fish and bear's meat had been cooked, were used as substitutes for chalk. (Our smaller illustration shows thirty-six syllabic characters with their names.)

After a few words of explanation the work of memorising the characters began.

A, E, Oo, Ah. It was just like a lot of little children in a primary school beginning with A, B, C. Over, and over again, we repeated them, one after the other, until my mixed audience became familiarised with the sounds. Thus we studied them for hours. At first the interest in the work was very great, and from the old men of eighty, to the boys and girls of six or eight the best of attention was paid. They seemed to vie with one another in their efforts to see which could master them most quickly.

After a time the interest flagged considerably, especially among the older men, as to them, these characters alone, were as yet, unmeaning sounds. Some of them got up and lit their pipes, and moving around, divided their time between the lesson and the smoking. Of course I had to let them smoke. I might have found it a difficult matter to have stopped them if I had been so foolish as to have tried. So I told them some pleasant stories, as we toiled on at our lesson, it was not many hours before a number of my undisciplined pupils had a fairly good idea of the names of the characters. Knowing that I could arouse the interest of the most apathetic among them when I began to combine the characters into words, I asked for their earnest attention while I proceeded in my work.

I marked out some simple words such as: (pa-pa,) (ma-ma,) (Oo-me-me,)—(English: pigeon.) I showed them how thus to combine these signs into words. This very much interested them; but the climax came, when with the burnt stick I marked (Maneto,—English: God, or the Great Spirit.) Great indeed was the excitement among them. They could hardly believe their own eyes that before them was Maneto, the Great Spirit. He whom they had heard in the thunder and the storm, whose power they had seen in the lightning flash, about whom, with reverence and awe, they had talked in their wigwams, and at their camp-fires— "Maneto!" Here, made by a burnt stick on a rock visible to their eyes, was that name: God on the Rock! It was indeed a revelation. Something that filled, and thrilled them, as I have never before or since seen Indians thrilled.

For a time I could only keep quiet and look on, and rejoice as I studied them. Some of them in their amazement were doubtful of their own senses. They acted as though they could not believe their own eyes; so they appealed to those nearest to them, and said:

"Is it Maneto to you?"

Others were noticed rubbing their eyes, as though they feared that by some witchery bad medicine had been thrown in them, and, in their Indian phraseology, they were "seeing double."

There was no more inattention. Every pipe went out, and every eye followed me, as in these syllables I wrote on the rock, God is Love. After talking about this a little. I then wrote, God Loves You. This we followed with other short sentences full of blessed Gospel truths. Thus passed some hours in this delightful way, and before they were ended, numbers of my pupils had become quite familiarised with the formation of words out of these characters.

Then we opened our bundle of Bibles, and, passing them around as far as they would go, I had them all turn to the first verse of the first chapter of Genesis. After some explanation of a few additional signs which they there saw upon the printed page, and which give some variation to the sound of the syllabic character to which they are attached, we began the study of the verse. Of course our progress at first was slow. It could not be otherwise under such circumstances. But we patiently persevered, and it was not very long ere they were able to read in their own language: "Ma-wache Nistum Kaesamaneto Keoosetou Kesik Mesa Askee, (In the beginning God created the heaven and the earth.")

When they had acquired the ability to read this verse for themselves, and had grasped a little of its meaning, there was another outburst of delight. That first verse of Genesis is very suggestive and full of meaning to any one, no matter how learned, who strives to investigate it. It is in itself the first chapter of God's revelation of Himself to man, and has long occupied the attention and study of the most godly and profound. Here, for the first time, it was being read by a company of poor Indians just emerging from paganism. But they were sharp and keen, and able to grasp a new truth; and so when the verse first opened before them with its wondrous meaning, great was their delight and amazement.

"Now we know all about it!" some of them shouted. "The Kaesa-Maneto, (the great God,) made all these things, the heaven and the earth."

Others said:

"Our fathers talked about it in their wigwams, and wondered how all these things came as they are; but they had to confess that they were in darkness, and knew nothing. But now we know it! We know it!"

Over and over again they read the verse until they had thoroughly committed it to memory. And in after days, at many a campfire and in many a hunting lodge, it was repeated to others who had not heard it, but who, on hearing it, were also filled with gratification and delight at the answer which it gave to what had long been a subject of perplexity and awe.

Day after day before that rock the study of other verses followed. Slowly of course at first, but gradually increasing as they became more and more acquainted with the syllabics. Thus these eager interested Indians, studied amidst these primitive surroundings, and applied themselves with such earnestness to their work, that although they had never been to school a day in their lives, some of them, in ten days or two weeks were able to read with fluency the Word of God in their own language. No wonder the great Lord Dufferin, then Governor General of the Dominion of Canada, said to me:

The man who invented that syllabic alphabet, was one of the great benefactors of humanity, and more richly deserved a pension, a title, and a resting place in Westminster Abbey, than many who were there buried.

For some years, at several of the missions, the Christian Indians were only taught a knowledge of these syllabic characters, and were thus only able to read the books which were printed with them. Now, however, in all the schools, the English language is taught also, and our common alphabet is in general use. The result is, that many of the younger generation understand, talk, and read in English. English Bibles are being circulated among them, and many of the younger people already prefer the English Bible to the Indian translation. Still, all the older people only understand the syllabic characters; and so for years to come, this wonderful invention will still be utilised, and will continue to be a benediction. Hymn-books, catechisms, the Pilgrim's Progress, and a few other books of a religious character, have been printed in the syllables, and are much prized and well used, by their Indian readers.

All the churches that are currying on missionary work in those vast northern regions have availed themselves of Mr Evans' invention. Among other tribes than the Cree, where there are different sounds in their language, some few extra characters have been added. Even in Labrador and Greenland the devoted Moravian missionaries who are there toiling, are successfully using the syllabic characters to teach the poor wandering Esquimaux how to read, in his own uncouth Language, the Word of God.

Chapter Six.

The Story of Sandy Harte.

Among all of my appointments, the one which perhaps
afforded me the greatest pleasure and satisfaction, was that
of Nelson River. At Oxford house we had a larger number
of converted Indians; but that mission had been long
organised, and devout and earnest men, like Reverend
Messrs Brooking, and Stringfellow, had given to it years of
honest self-denying toil. Nelson River, on the other hand,
was a new and untried field, where it was my privilege and
joy to go as the first missionary.

Of the many grand converts there happily rescued from the
darkness and power of paganism, there is one beautiful
character who is now the right hand of the resident
missionary. His name is Sandy Harte. My introduction to
him was a peculiar one. The day was one of rare beauty,
and I had spent the forenoon in teaching a number of adults
and Indian children how to read the Word of God printed in
the syllabic characters. During the noon hour of rest I
entered the birch bark wigwam of one of the principal
Indians, and was naturally surprised to observe a fine
looking Indian lad stretched out on a bed of rabbit robes
and blankets while the other boys were engaged in various
sports. Addressing him, I said:

"Why are you lying here this beautiful day?"

With a sudden movement he jerked away the upper robe
that was over him, and, pointing to his shattered thigh, said
in tones full of bitterness:

"Missionary, that is the reason why I am here, instead of being out in the sunshine with the other boys."

The despairing tone, the emphatic utterance, at once aroused my sympathies and caused me to be deeply interested in this wounded boy, so helpless, not knowing the hour when, according to the prevailing custom, he might be put to death. The heartless reasoning of these Indians in such cases was like this: he will always be lame and helpless; why should he be a burden on his friends? let us kill him at once; it will be better for him and them. However, they had postponed the killing of this lad because he was the son of the chief.

After I had examined his wound and had given some directions as to its treatment, I sat down beside him and heard from his lips the sad story of the misfortune which had crippled him for life. It seems, that he and another boy were out shooting partridges and rabbits. While moving through the forest, Sandy walking ahead, the gun of his comrade accidentally went off and poured its contents into his leg. The bone was badly splintered, and the muscles so cut and torn, that there was absolutely no possibility of his ever being able to walk on it again.

After I had had quite a chat with him, I asked if he would like to be able to read the Word of God. His bright eyes shone with pleasure, and his response was so expressive of eager longing, that I at once began the first lesson. Sitting beside him on the ground, I drew the syllabic characters and spent an hour or so in teaching them to him. He had a very retentive memory, and was intensely anxious to learn as rapidly as possible. So, every day, when I had finished giving lessons to the crowd of young and old people, I used to hurry over to the wigwam where he lay to give him additional instruction; and so deeply interested was he, that I felt well repaid for my trouble.

As I was hundreds of miles from home—having come on that long trail with a couple of Indians in a birch canoe—and had a number of other points at which I wished to stop and do missionary work, I was obliged to bring my visit at this place to an end after a couple of weeks. But before leaving, I had an informal conversation with Murdo, Oowikapun, and some other of the friendly Indians.

"What a pity it is," I exclaimed, "that Sandy could not be educated! If only he could be educated enough to be your teacher, what a good thing it would be! For, next to a missionary to live permanently among you, a godly teacher would be the best thing you could have. He will never again have the full use of his leg, so will not be able to become a great hunter; but if he had an education, he might be a blessing to you all!"

Then I bade farewell to these northern Indians who had received me so kindly, and with some parting words, especially urging that the wounded boy should be kindly cared for, I resumed my adventurous journey.

As we journeyed on from place to place we had plenty of strange adventures. We shot a fine black bear, and, at our first meal after our battle with him, enjoyed picking his ribs. In his capture, I was very much interested in watching how human experience was able to overmatch animal instinct. We had a very narrow escape in some wild and treacherous rapids, where we lost part of the contents of our canoe and were all nearly drowned ere we succeeded in reaching the shore. This loss was the more keenly felt, as in such an isolated place it is utterly impossible to replenish your store. However, after several such mishaps, we succeeded in carrying out our programme; and at length reached home in safety.

The long winter, with its seven or eight months of bitter cold, set in shortly after. For a few weeks I was kept busy with home matters and the affairs of the local mission appointment. As soon, however, as the great lakes and rivers were well frozen over and a sufficient fall of snow made it possible to begin my winter journeys, I harnessed my dogs, and with my guide and dog-drivers, responded, as far as possible, to the many calls to tell the Story of the Great Book.

So many were the Macedonian calls from other places that winter, that I did not make a trip to Nelson River. This I regretted exceedingly, for although it was the most distant, it was one of the most promising and encouraging of all the new fields to which I had gone.

About the middle of the following summer, while enjoying the glories of a magnificent sunset, I saw a canoe with some Indians in it coming toward our home. When they had landed, two of them at once came up to me, greeted me most cordially, and before I could fully return their greetings, or recall where I had before seen them, exclaimed:

"We remember your good words to us—and we have brought Sandy along."

"Sandy along! Who is Sandy?" I asked.

"Why, Sandy Harte—you remember him—the boy who was shot in the leg—the one you used to go and teach; we have brought him along, for we remember your words, so sweet to us, about him."

"What were my words?" I asked, for I could not at that moment recall them.

"Why, your words were: What a pity it is that Sandy is not educated! If he were educated, he might be such a blessing to you all. We have not forgotten it. We have often talked about it. What you said to us and taught us from the Great Book was so good, we are hungry for more. We are willing to be taught. You cannot come all the time. We want some one to be with us who knows something; so we have brought Sandy all the way in the canoe to be taught by you; and then, to come back to us, that we may learn of him."

There was no mistake about it. There was Sandy in the middle of the canoe looking up at me with those brilliant black eyes that had so attracted me in that wigwam far away.

I went down to the canoe, spoke kindly to the lad, shook his hand, and invited all the Indians into my house.

After introducing them to my good wife, I told her Sandy's story; and how they had remembered my words of a year ago, and had brought him on this long journey to place him in our care: utterly unable themselves to do anything for his support, I confess, that for the moment, I regretted having been so quick in uttering words which had been so construed, by these Indians and which had thrown upon our care this wild wounded Indian boy.

It was the time of the first Riel Rebellion in Manitoba, and although we were living far north of the actual scene of rebellion, yet our supplies had in so great a measure been cut off, that we were existing on very scant rations. Often we averaged no more than two meals a day, and frequently, when eating breakfast, we did not know from what quarter our dinner was to come. And now while on the verge of starvation, came this extraordinary addition to our family, which meant another mouth to feed, and another body to clothe. In our abounding poverty, here indeed was a trial of faith!

After talking the matter over with my brave large-hearted wife, and asking divine direction, the noble woman said:

"The Lord is in it, and He who has sent the mouth to be filled will surely send all our additional requirements."

So we cheerfully received Sandy into our home and made him as one of our family. He was in a deplorable condition in more ways than one. Coming from a wild band of Indians who were in complete ignorance of cleanliness and of the habits and requirements of the whites, this poor wounded Indian boy had many things to learn; and at first, on account of his ignorance and prejudices, we had many opportunities for the exercise of patience and forbearance.

How Sandy was conquered.

Like nearly all of the pagan Indians, Sandy had prejudices against women, and it was hard at first to get him to pay any attention to what the missionary's wife said. He thought it humiliating and degrading to obey, or even to pay any attention to a woman's request. Yet we both treated him with the greatest kindness, and hoped and prayed, that time and the grace of God would work the changes needed for him.

He was a bright scholar and made rapid progress in his studies, and in a few months was able to read in his own language. For a time, the novelty of his new surroundings kept him interested, and he seemed quite at home. He made many friends among our Christian Indians, who, on learning of the peculiar way in which he had been thrown upon our hands, became much interested in him. He went to Sunday school, and also attended the various services in the church; but for a long time it seemed as though it was only in the spirit of mere idle curiosity, or because others did so.

When the first long winter after his arrival had ended, and the springtime had come again, Sandy became very homesick and longed to go back to his far-off wigwam abode. The sight of rippling waters and running streams was too much for his wild untamed spirit, and he chafed under the discipline of a civilised home, and became dejected and miserable. We all noticed his restlessness; but talked kindly to him, and urged him to apply himself to his lessons, that he might the sooner be able to return to his wild free life in his distant home. But Indian-like, the more we said to him, the worse he seemed to become, until he made it very uncomfortable for us all.

One day instead of going to school, he hobbled away on his crutches to a picturesque point of land which jutted far out into the lake. In the evening, the teacher came to the mission house and inquired why Sandy had not been at school that day. This of course was news to us. We were at once much alarmed, and immediately began searching for the absentee. After about an hour's search, in which quite a number of Indians took part, Sandy was found curled up among the rocks on the point, crying bitterly for his Nelson River home.

Having exhausted all my persuasive powers, I saw that I must change my style of dealing with him. So, appearing to be very indignant, I picked up a large stick, and, rushing at him, sternly ordered him to get up and return to our house as quickly as possible. With a frightened glance into my face to see how much I meant, he sprang up and hurried back to the mission house, I gave him a severe reprimanding, asking him, among other things if he thought such conduct on his part was a fair return for all our kindness to him. Then I said to him sharply:

"Go up to your room and bring down all your torn and soiled clothes and moccasins."

With a sad look he obeyed, and soon returned with his bundle. After looking over the lot, I took them away from him; and, calling in an Indian woman, gave her some soap and sewing material, and told her to take all of those things, wash and mend them nicely, bring them back to me, and I would pay her for her trouble. When he saw his clothes going away, he was in great perplexity and distress as he was not at all sure that they would be returned to him. The fact was, he had a good deal of vanity about him in those days, and I made the discovery that he had become very proud of the clothes we had given him in place of the wretched ones in which he had been brought to us. So, the threatened loss of all he had except what he wore, was to him a dire calamity, I let him grieve for some hours, saying but little to him, resolved to put a stop to his nonsense which was only making himself and others miserable.

When the bundle of clean clothing returned, I added to it new pants, shirts, moccasins, a bright handkerchief, and a hat; then, in the kindest way possible, with loving words. I gave him the whole bundle. Poor boy! he was bewildered and amazed. He could not speak his thanks; but his glistening tear dimmed eyes told us that he was cured and conquered. Never did the stern lesson have to be repeated.

But he was greatly perplexed. It was such different treatment from that to which he had been accustomed. This combination of sternness and kindness, was to him such a mystery, that he evidently could not stop thinking and wondering about it. So, one day when he had nothing to do, he went over to have a talk on the subject with one of the Indians who was a sensible Christian man and a great friend of his.

"I cannot make out our missionary," said Sandy. "When he came after me to the point where I had hid, he seemed very angry, and took up a big stick as if to strike me. Indeed, he nearly frightened the life out of me although he did not once hit me. Then, after ordering me back to the house in such a hurry, he made me bring out all my clothes, and gave them to a woman to carry away. Of course I never expected to see them again: but I did—they came back clean and mended, and he had added a lot more to them. I cannot understand it. The missionary at first seemed as though he would thrash me, then he turned round and gave me all these good things."

From the Christian Indian to whom Sandy had gone, we afterward learned all about this interview. He said he let the lad tell him of his perplexities, and then gave him a long faithful talk. Here is the substance of his reply to Sandy.

"The missionary and his kind wife have come here to do us good. They have left their friends far away. They were many days on their journey to this land, and have suffered many hardships. When your friends brought you here, they took you into their home and treated you, not as a servant, but as one of their own family. There is not an Indian in the village but would be glad to change places with you, and to be treated as you have been. If they have food, they share it equally with you. You have had medicine and bandages for your sore leg. You are well dressed. They have been like parents to you. Yet you have not been grateful. You acted very foolishly. You ran away from school and hid yourself. You made their hearts alarmed for fear some serious accident had happened to you. The worst is, you do not obey Ookemasquao (the missionary's wife,) as you ought. White ladies are to be as much obeyed and respected as men. Yet in spite of all your foolishness and stubbornness, they have been very patient with you. They kept hoping, that as you grew older you would grow wiser; but you have been getting so much worse lately, that the missionary has had to deal sternly with you. He, however, felt sorry for you; his heart was kind toward you all the time; and so, when you went back, he showed his love to you by his presents. We all see, that the missionary and his wife have nothing in their hearts toward you but love. But you must be obedient, and you ought to be thankful. They are praying much for you, and hoping that you will yet become a good Christian, and at some future time, be a great blessing to your own people."

Thus this sensible Christian Indian talked to Sandy, and it was to him a revelation. From that day there was a decided change in him for the better. He became obedient and studious, and was ever anxious to do what he could in return for the kindnesses shown to him. He was a capital shot, and he and I had some fine bunting and fishing excursions together. As his lameness interfered with successful hunting on land, but not with his dexterity in handling the paddle, I purchased for him a light canoe in which he made many short excursions.

Like all Indian boys, he was very clever with the bow and arrow. I remember an exhibition, of his quickness and skill that almost amazed me. I had taken him with me on a shooting excursion to a place which was called the Old Fort. It was so named from the fact, that many years before, the Hudson Bay Company had a trading post there for traffic with the Indians. It had been abandoned for many years, but in its vicinity were some capital hunting grounds. This spot to which Sandy and I had gone for ducks, was about twenty miles from our home. We had paddled that distance in our canoe, and were quite successful in replenishing our larder. While carefully paddling along, we saw a fine large mallard duck swimming quite a distance ahead. When we thought we were within range, Sandy, who was in the bow of the canoe, carefully raised his gun and fired. Whether it was owing to the movement of the canoe or not I cannot say; but he missed the duck. Quick as a flash he threw down his gun, and, catching up his bow and arrow, fired at the duck which of course had instantly risen, and was flying away directly in front of us. Imagine my surprise and delight, to see the arrow wing its way so unerringly, that it pierced the duck, and brought it suddenly down into the river.

Thus Sandy not only became a wiser and a better boy, but at times he was quite helpful in his way, and returned from some hunting excursions with quite a variety of small game which added considerably to our household bill of fare. We praised him for his skill and industry and very quickly discovered, that kind loving words were the highest reward which could be given him. Poor boy! he had had but few of them in paganism; and now from us, whom he had learned to respect and love, they were as water to a thirsty soul.

## Sandy's Conversion.

About a year after this unpleasantness with Sandy, a very gracious revival began among our Indians, extending far and wide. It was the fruit of years of teaching and preaching by numbers of devoted missionaries, and of much personal effort to bring the people to a decision for Christianity. I had observed with great joy, that the prayer-meetings and other social religious services, were largely increased by the attendance of Indians who had been under religious influences for a long time, but had not yet fully given themselves to Christ. Even among the pagan Indians there was less opposition to Christianity, and a greater willingness to hear the Word than ever before. At times this spirit showed itself in a way that to most people would have seemed to savour much of selfishness. For example, one day, very early in the morning, the chief came rushing into our mission house, and gave utterance to this extraordinary statement:

"Missionary, there are a lot of pagan Indians at the Fort. They are the ones you were talking to about becoming Christians. I have just come from visiting them, and have been urging them to give up their old way; they said to me, 'Tell your missionary, if he will give us one good square meal of potatoes, we will come and hear him preach three times!'"

Doubtless many will smile at this quaint offer—this queer exchange of commodities; yet we who were on the ground, and remembered the haughty stubborness of those same Indians only a short time before, were glad to hear thus from them. We promptly accepted the challenge and furnished the potatoes. What appetites they had! But they carried out their share of the contract, and listened attentively—and smoked—during the three services. They were always friendly afterward; and, in subsequent years, a number of them became sincere Christians. It pays to get the truth into the heart, even if we have to begin by filling the stomach with potatoes!

So anxious had Sandy become to win our approval, that we knew he was willing and courageous enough to take any stand we suggested. But we were so very anxious that his decision for Christ should be built on a deeper, firmer foundation than a mere desire to please us, that, in talking with him, we used no special personal persuasion to bring him to a decision for the Lord Jesus. It was evident to us by his life that the Good Spirit was graciously working upon his heart, and that he was under deep religious conviction.

And soon the blessed hour came. One afternoon, while I was urging upon the large audience who had assembled in the church the privilege and necessity of immediate decision for Christ, Sandy, with others, sprang up from his seat near the door and came forward for prayer. His first audible petition still rings in my ear as though uttered but yesterday:

"O Tapa-yechekayan Kiss-awa-totawenan!" (Oh Lord, have mercy upon me!)

I knelt beside him and pointed him to the dear Saviour—
the sinners Friend. I quoted the sweet promises of the
blessed Book, and assured him they were for him. He wept,
and was deeply anxious for the assurance that even, he had
a personal interest in the crucified One. Earnest prayers
were offered for him and others, who, like him, were
seeking the Pearl of great price. We talked to him of the
love of God as revealed in Jesus. We tried to explain to him
the way of faith—the simple plan of salvation. That best of
all Teachers, that infallible Guide, the Holy Spirit, applied
the truth to his heart; and our dear Sandy saw the way, and
believed unreservedly in the Lord Jesus. He was a sweet
singer, and had often joined with us in our songs of
devotion at our family altar; but now as never before he
sang in his own musical language the translation of the
verse "My God is reconciled," etcetera.

"Ma' to noo-too-ta-min

Ne-pa-tan a-e-sit,

Ak-wa a-wa-ko-mit

Na-ma-ne-say-ke-sin,

Wa-na-tuk-ne-pa-hi-to-tan

Abba No-ta a-e-tae-yan."

Need we add that our Indian boy, so strangely thrown on
our care, was doubly dear and precious to as from that
hour! We had had our long months of trouble and anxiety
about him, and friends, both white and Indian, had thought,
and had told us, that what we were doing for him was,

"love's labour lost." How thankful we were at this glad hour of his clear and beautiful conversion, that we had persevered? We never could help feeling that his coming to us was from God, and in spite of all the discouragements, we had not dared to give up our charge. We had accepted it as a trust although it became a trial of patience; yet when the clouds cleaved away, we had our exceeding great reward.

From that day, his presence in our humble mission home was a benediction. He became a very devout and reverent student of the Word of God; and as its blessed truths opened up before him, he had many questions to ask, so that we had many loving talks about the holy Book. Often his heart overflowed with gratitude and thanksgiving to God, and he would exclaim—

"O missionary, these words are very sweet to my heart!"

To spend hours on his knees with his open Bible before him, was no uncommon thing for Sandy. And when he came down from his upper room with his face radiant, he would sometimes exclaim:

"Oh, how blind and stupid I was! I used to think that the white man's religion was just like the Indian's, only performed in another way, but now I know—yes I know it is different: oh so different! For do I not feel it in my heart, that God is my Father, and His Son is my Saviour, my Elder Brother! Oh yes, I know! I know!"

Then he would burst into song, asking us to join with him, which we often did gladly; and heaven seemed nearer while we sang.

Thus, he lived with us as a son in our home. He studied hard, and grew physically and spiritually. His faith never wavered, and his simple trust never gave way to doubt. He was a benediction in the schoolroom, and the transformation of a number of wild Indian lads into loving, docile pupils, was the result of his kindly influence over them.

The long cold winter came and passed away. During it I travelled some thousands of miles on my dog-sleds, or tramped through, the deep snow, day after day, on my snow shoes. Among other places, I visited Nelson River, and had the great pleasure of taking down some little gifts from Sandy to his relatives.

The following summer, I again visited his people and had the joy of telling them, that he was well and was making rapid progress in his studies. Great was their rejoicings at this good news.

On these trips we had our usual amount of hardships and dangers, and met with some peculiar adventures. One that very much interested us all, and for a time much excited me, was our discovery of a bear fishing, and our capture of his supplies. He was a fine large black fellow, and had seated himself on a rock near the shore. Between this rock and the shore rushed a little portion of the great river, in which quite a shoal of white fish seemed to have been spawning. The sharp eyes of the bear having detected them, he had resolved to capture a number of them for his supper. His hand-like paw was all the fishing tackle he needed. He very skilfully thrust it low down into the water under the passing fish, and with a sudden movement sent the finny beauty flying through the air, and out upon the not very distant shore. When our canoe appeared around a bend in the river, his fine sense of hearing detected our approach. At first, he seemed to show fight, and acted as though he would defend his fish; but a bullet caused him to change his mind about fighting, and he fled into the forest leaving us to enjoy his splendid fish. Good fish indeed they were, and quite sufficient for our evening and morning meals, in spite of the good appetites which such a glorious out-of-door life had given us.

## Sandy, a Benediction.

The next summer after Sandy's conversion, my good wife and I noticed, that for several days he was restless and excited, and, to use an Indian phrase, there was something on his mind. We kindly questioned him as to the cause of his unrest and mental disquietude, and drew from him, that it was solely on account of a visit that was soon to be paid him by quite a number of the trip men of his own Nelson River people. His anxiety was, that at this the first meeting with his own people since he had become a Christian, the talk which he was going to give them on the subject of the good Book and his acceptance of Christianity, might be made a great blessing to them.

So many and so valuable were the furs obtained in those days in the Nelson River district, that often two brigades of boats were necessary to bring up the catch of the previous winter. If the missionaries have been preaching the Gospel at the different posts where these brigades are made up, in all probability, part of the people have accepted Christianity, while others still walk in their own ways. On their trips, the Christians naturally travel together, while the pagans, selecting one of their own party as their leader, form a separate brigade.

It was known, that the first brigade coming consisted principally of those who had as yet refused to renounce their pagan ways. Among them were some of Sandy's own relatives, and he was intensely anxious, that they should no longer continue in their opposition to Christianity, and when appealed to on the subject, shrug their shoulders and say:

"As our fathers lived and died, so will we."

So we found out that the cause of Sandy's restlessness was his great anxiety to help these, his friends, to know the Christ.

With glad hearts we cheerfully promised to aid him all we could. Still he lingered, and it was evident that something else was on his mind, although he had very warmly expressed his gratitude for our promise of assistance. We encouraged him to tell us what was still on his heart, so that if possible we might help him. Cheered by our words he said:

"Oh! I know you will help me to tell them of Jesus and His love; but you know that most of these boatmen are not yet Christians, and they are so blind and stupid. They are just like I was in my ignorance of this religion—of the Bible; and my trouble and fear is that when I begin to talk to them of this blessed way, they will get up and leave before I have had time to say all that there is in my heart. I am afraid we cannot keep them together unless—unless—"

"Unless what?" I said as he stopped.

The dear fellow looked up in our faces, and, seeing nothing but encouragement there, mustered up courage to say this that was in his heart:

"Unless we give them something to eat."

We had been long enough among the Indians to know that the boy was right; for often, to win the poor ignorant creatures and bring them within sound of the Gospel, had we given them even the food from our own table, until we ourselves knew what genuine hunger was. Then we could better understand, how difficult it was for poor hungry listeners to give undivided attention to spiritual exhortations on an empty stomach.

"Of course you shall have a dinner for them, Sandy," said my brave wife, "and we will do the best we can afford for you and your people."

His cup of happiness seemed full, as he heard this answer, and as we saw the clouds flitting away, I said:

"Is this what has been troubling you for days?"

"Yes," he replied, "what right have I to ask such a favour from you who have been so kind to me? You let me come into your house when I was wounded, and dark, and wicked; clothed me, and have even treated me as though I had been your son; and best of all, you have led me up into this great joy of knowing that I am a child of God."

Here his eyes filled and he was overcome by deep emotion. Much moved, we waited silently until he had controlled himself, when he continued:

"You know how every day we have together prayed for my people; and when alone before God I pray for them; they are always in my heart and prayers; and now that I am to have the chance of speaking to them, I do want it to succeed. You know, that the poor pagan Indian seems better able, or more willing, somehow, to listen after he has had something to eat."

So it was settled to Sandy's great delight, that when his friends arrived from Nelson River they were to be invited to the mission house for dinner.

It was a beautiful day when they came. A long table had been made and put up on the grassy lawn in front of the house, and a good substantial meal had been prepared. Fortunately, our supply boat had arrived from Red River, and some Indian hunters had brought in abundance of game, so that we had enough and to spare, even for a crowd of Indians.

Sandy was full of bliss. To watch him, and to observe how interested his people were in him, gave us great delight.

He seated his Indian friends to suit his own mind, for his thoughts were more on the after service than on the substantial meal before them. When all were in their assigned places, he said:

"Now, wait a minute. From the Great Spirit we receive all our blessings; so shut your eyes while I thank Him and ask His blessing upon us."

They obeyed readily: for was he not the son of a chief, and taught of the missionary? They did not know what "Amen" meant, so, after Sandy had said it, still kept their eyes shut, and had to be told to open them and begin at their dinners.

They had a good time together. There was nothing rude or awkward in any of their actions, and a stranger looking on, would never have imagined that the majority of these polite, courteous, yet picturesquely garbed bronzed stalwart men, had never before sat at a table or eaten with forks. These latter are considered superfluous in the Indian country. Give an Indian a good knife and a horn or wooden spoon—and what cares he for a fork? His only concern is in reference to the supply of food. But on this occasion we had placed forks at each place, and after those who had never seen them before had observed how one familiar with them used his, they all quickly imitated him and did exceedingly well.

What appetites they had! It was a pleasure to see how they enjoyed their dinner—especially as we knew that we had enough for all.

### Sandy, a Missionary.

When dinner was ended, and they were about to rise from the table, a few words from Sandy caused them all to remain quietly seated. Now we perceived, why he had arranged them at the table as he did. Every one was so seated that he could easily see, as well as hear. It was evident that they were all very much interested, and full of curiosity to hear the message he had for them.

They were doubtless well aware, that such a feast as had been prepared for them meant a talk at the close; but none of them ever dreamed that Sandy—"their Sandy"—was to be the principal speaker. When at the close he so naturally and ably took control, they were at first amazed, and then delighted, that one of their own people—and a young man at that—was not only able to do such a thing, but was encouraged in the undertaking by the missionary and his wife.

Fearing that our presence might embarrass Sandy, my wife and I moved our chairs back a little behind him, but still near enough to hear all that was said. We were intensely interested in the proceedings, and lifted up our hearts to God that divine help and guidance might be given to the one whom we now loved to call "our Sandy."

A little nervousness that was at first noticeable, disappeared after a few sentences, and then, with a fluency and eloquence that simply amazed us, the loving burning words flowed from his lips. With few words of explanation he took up his beloved Bible and hymn-book, and began the service.

Of the actual words of that address, I can now recall very few; but the memory of it will live forever. He told them the story of his life from the time when, having found my way to their distant land, I met him in his wigwam home as he lay wounded upon the ground, talked kindly to him, and gave him his first lesson. He spoke of his long, long journey in the canoe, and of his arrival at our home. He described how kindly he had been received, how stupidly and ungratefully he had acted when the novelty of the new way of living had worn off, and how he had been so foolish as to long for his old life in the wigwam. He denounced in very emphatic language, his own ingratitude toward us for

all the kindness we had shown him and the patience with
which we had borne with his stupidity.

Then he told the story of his conversion: would that I could
tell it as he did! He contrasted their old foolish religion of
the conjurers—which had only kept them in fear and terror
all their days, bringing no peace or rest to their souls—with
that which was taught in the blessed Book; which had come
as a great joy into his life, filling him with peace in the
assurance that even he was a child of God. He had his date
in his spiritual life—his well remembered birthday; and to
it he referred. He told of that afternoon in the church, when,
in response to the invitation: "Who will give his heart to
God to-day?" he had answered, "I will!" and bowing down
before God in prayer, had sought for the forgiveness of his
sins and the assurance of the divine favour. Very clearly,
and with much emotion he assured them that, while trusting
and believing that Jesus Christ, the Son of God, was able
and willing to receive him, He had indeed received him.

Thus in earnest tones, in his beautiful Indian tongue, he
went on and on; now, urging and exhorting them to accept
of this great salvation from the Great Spirit who was the
loving Father of all, and who desired the salvation of every
one of His children whether they were white or Indian; and
then, again referring to his own conversion and the joy that
had come to him, as one reason why he wished them all to
be Christians.

Mrs Young and I were delighted and also amazed; not only
at his readiness of utterance, but at the religious character
and power of the address. I could only say in my heart:

"This is the outcome of those long hours which this young
child of God has spent day after day with the open Book

before him and the Holy Spirit as his teacher; and, thank God, here is the glorious reward for all we have had to do for, and bear with this wild unkempt Indian lad. In this one glad hour we see enough amply to repay us for all we have had to put up with ere there was the first appreciation of our kindness. It has seemed a long time between the seed sowing and the reaping; but the harvest time has come at last and here we witness this glorious sight—Sandy, our once wild rebellious Indian boy, now with radiant face and eloquent tongue, in most beautiful and scriptural language, urging and beseeching his Indian friends to renounce their old foolish paganism and to accept of Christianity."

As he talked the faces of his Indian auditors were indeed studies. They were literally drinking in his marvellous words. To a few of them I had preached on some of my long journeys; but beside these few, there were those now listening to Sandy who had never heard such things before, and they seemed amazed and confounded. Persons who have never witnessed it, can hardly imagine the astonishment, and sometimes awe, that fails over a company of pure pagans, when, for the first time, the story of Redeeming Love is heard.

Sandy went on to tell them of his love and anxiety for them, and of his desire and constant prayers that they should all become Christians, and know for themselves that God loved them and that they were His children. He explained to them, how, at first, he thought the Bible was only for the white man; but that he had learned, that the Great Spirit has given His Book to all races, loving all alike. This was the reason he was so anxious that his own people should accept this great salvation which was for them. It would make them happy, as it was making others everywhere who fully accepted it.

They listened to the end of his long address with intense interest. In response to his request, a number of questions were asked in reference to this new way, and how it was possible for them to enter into it. His answers were very appropriate and beautiful. In addition to his own words, he again opened his Bible and read promise after promise to them, to show the universality of the love of God, and that he had given his Son to die for them all, and what they must do to receive this love into their hearts.

At his request, I followed with a short address, endorsing what he had said. I lovingly entreated them to remember his words, and to do as he had done—give their hearts to God; and thus become His happy, loving children. A hymn was sung; earnest prayers were offered up; the benediction was pronounced—and this remarkable service came to an end.

Ere they departed they gathered around Sandy and kissed him. They asked him more questions about this new way, and with some of them he had earnest faithful talks. They all came and shook hands with us, and very kindly thanked us for our great love and kindness to their Ookemasis,—the young chief,—as they now laughingly called Sandy.

After remaining with us some years, Sandy returned to his own land and people. Among them he still lives a devoted, industrious Christian. He is the right-hand man of the missionary, a blessing and a benediction to many, and we count it as one of our "chief joys" that we were instrumental in leading him into the light.

## Chapter Seven.

## The New Year's Indian Feast.

From time immemorial the Indians have been noted for the
number of their feasts. Some of these—as the New Moon
and the First-Fruits of the corn, celebrated, by a part of the
tribes—were generally innocent, seeming to point to some
Jewish origin in the dim past; others—such as the feast of
the dogs when the poor animals were wantonly torn to
pieces—were loathsome in the extreme.

As soon as the missionaries succeeded in getting the red
men to listen to the Gospel, they insisted upon the
suppression of the sinful feasts; especially as they were
more or less associated with their ideas of worship. Even
the dog feast was considered "good medicine" to propitiate
the evil spirits: for the dogs were prized by the Indian next
to his children, and sacrificing them was making a very
great offering.

When the missionaries went among the Northern Wood
Crees, they met with a great degree of success in winning
the people from their pagan superstitions. They, of course,
insisted upon the entire giving up of all the objectionable
habits and customs of their past life; and among them, their
sinful feasts. However, they did not try to root the word out
of their language; but as a substitute for what was so
wrong, organised a Christian festival. This great feast was
celebrated on New Year's day—unless that day happened
to fall on Sunday, when it was held on the day following—
at Norway House, the largest mission station in those days.

Preparations for it were begun many months in advance. A great Indian council would be held at which, as a mere formality, the question would be first asked: "Are we to have the great feast this year?"

This would be carried unanimously, and—for Indians— with great applause. The next question which required more time for answering would be: "What is each man prepared to give as his contribution toward the feast?"

Very strange at first seemed the answers. Mamanowatum, a big Indian moose-hunter, would say:

"I have discovered the trail of a moose. I will give half of the animal—and his nose."

The moose nose is considered a great delicacy. Moose meat is the best of all venison; and Mamanowatum was a most successful hunter. So this splendid contribution, although the moose had yet to be shot, and was hard to kill, would be recorded with great pleasure.

Then Soquatum would say; "I have discovered a bear's den. I will give half the bear to the feast—and all the paws."

This generous contribution would also meet with much approval, for the beat's paws are likewise among the great delicacies of the country.

Mustagan would speak next, and would say; "I know where there is a large beaver house, and I will give five beavers— and ten tails."

This donation would also meet with great satisfaction, as beavers are capital eating, and their great broad tails, together with the moose's nose and the bear's paws, constitute the principal delicacies of the country.

Rapidly would the hunters rise up one after another and proffer their gifts, keeping the Indian secretary busily employed in writing down in syllabic characters, the various promised offerings of game, the greater quantity of which would be still roaming—perhaps hundreds of miles away—in the wintry forest.

Those among the hunters who excelled in catching the valuable fur-bearing animals, whose flesh is worthless for food, would make their contribution in rich furs, such as minks, martins, otters and ermines, which would be exchanged in the Hudson Bay Company's stores for flour, tea, sugar and plums.

The council would last until all who could give, or had any remote idea of success, had recorded their contributions.

Shortly after would begin the work of securing the promised offerings for the feast. Even the successful ones did not always bring in what they had promised. Sometimes those who had promised beaver, would be so fortunate as to meet with a herd of reindeer, and thus would return with their contribution in venison, perhaps four times in excess of the beaver promised. Or perhaps the man who promised a couple of wildcats—and they are not bad eating—while out diligently searching for them, would detect the tiny ascending thread of vapoury steam from a great snowdrift, which told him, that low down there in a den were sleeping some fat hears. These would be dug out, and killed, and part of the meat would be brought in to the feast. Again it

sometimes happened—as hunter's luck is very uncertain—
that some who promised a large contribution were not able
to bring so much. However, with the donations from the
fur-traders and the mission house, there would be a large
supply: and this was necessary, as Indians have good
appetites.

As the different kinds of animals were shot or captured, the
meat would be brought to the mission, and well secured
from cunning dogs in the large fish-house; where it would
freeze solid, and so keep in good condition until required.
About a week before the day of the feast, the missionary's
wife would call to her assistance a small number of clever
Indian women; and, aided by some men who would cut the
frozen meat into pieces of suitable size, they would roast or
boil the whole of this great assortment. It was an
"assortment," and proudly would they look at it, and
rejoice. Out of the flour, plums, sugar and bear's grease—a
substitute for suet—great plum-puddings would be made,
hard and solid; but the chunks cut off with an axe, gave
much satisfaction to the hearty eaters.

When the day arrived, preparations for the feast began very
early. The seats were removed from the church, and tables
the whole length of the interior, were quickly made and put
in position by the native carpenters. Great roaring fires
were built in the two iron stoves, and the inside
temperature of the building made as nearly tropical as
possible; while outside it was fifty degrees below zero, or
even colder. This intense heat was necessary to thaw out
the meat, which, after it had been cooked a day or two
before, had quickly cooled and frozen solid. The great
supply was soon carried into the hot church, and after the
few hours that elapsed before the feast began, it was in
capital condition for the twelve or fifteen hundred hungry

Indian who for weeks had been eagerly looking forward to
this great event.

They were a motley company, all welcome, and all in the
best of humour. Chiefs and head men were receiving
directions from the missionary, transmitting them to the
workers, and seeing that everything was done. Happy busy
women, under the loving guidance of the missionary's
wife, whom they simply idolised, were arranging the tables,
for the equipment of which, all the table necessaries of the
village,—principally tin cups and plates,—as well as of the
mission pantry, were brought into service. Great boilers
and kettles of tea were brewed, and hundreds of flat cakes,
made of flour, water and a little salt, were baked in frying
pans or on top of the stoves, cut into large pieces, and made
ready for distribution.

While busy hands were thus employed in making these
final arrangements for the great feast, which generally
began about one o'clock, the hundreds of other Indians—
especially the young men—were having various sports
outside. The toboggan slides of the schoolboys had many
visitors; and some lively games of football were played on
the frozen lake. The snow had been scraped away from a
smooth hit of ice where the active skaters showed their
speed and skill. But the thoughts of all were on the feast,
and they were anxious for the sound of the bell that would
summon them to its enjoyment.

About the middle of the forenoon, there was a most
interesting break in the preparations. The chief would go to
the missionary and ask for a pencil and piece of writing
paper. Then, taking with him one of the principal men into
the church, where the crowd of workers were busily

engaged, he would call for a short halt in the proceedings, and standing on a bench, ask:

"How many of our people are sick, or aged, or wounded, and are thus unable to be with us at the great feast to-day? Give me their names."

As the names were mentioned, they would be recorded; until, perhaps, twenty or more were thus called out.

"Any more?" the chief would cry. "Let none be overlooked on this happy day."

"Oh yes, there is an old bed-ridden woman, lying on her couch of rabbit skins and balsam boughs, in a wigwam six miles up Jack River," says one.

"I heard, that there are two sick people left behind in a wigwam on the island over near York village by the pagan Indians who have come to the feast," says another.

"Put them down, of course. But stop! One of you go out and ask those who have come, if there are not more than those two left behind."

Soon word comes in that there are not only these two sick ones, but a little girl with a broken leg.

"Put her name down, too."

The list is again read over, and the question again asked:

"Are you sure that we have not overlooked any? It would be a shame for us to be here feasting and any of our aged and afflicted ones forgotten."

The matter would be discussed until they were confident that all the names were recorded, even the afflicted ones of the still unconverted Indians who were always welcomed and generally on hand. Then the chief, with an assistant or two would go to the great piles of food, and cut off generous pieces of venison and bear's meat, and, with an assortment of other things, make up as many large parcels as there were names on his list, each bundle, perhaps, containing enough food to last the afflicted ones a couple of days. Then the chief would go out to where the sturdy active young men were at their sports, and shouting the names of as many as he had bundles, give to the fleetest a large bundle and say:

"Take that to Ookoominou, who Is sick in bed six miles up the river, and tell her that we are all sorry that she is so old and feeble that she cannot be with us to-day. With it give her our Christian greetings and love, and our wishes that she will enjoy her share of the feast."

With a look to see that the strings of his moccasins and his beaded garters are well tied, and tightening his sash belt around his leathern shirt, the swift runner would be off like an arrow; making straight for the far away wigwam, where, in age and feebleness, is one of the grandmothers of the tribe, now loved by all; but who would have been put to death years ago, if the blessed Gospel had not come among this people and wrought its marvellous transformations in their hearts. Six miles would that fleet Indian runner have to go, and return, ere he could have his share of the feast; but never fear, he will be back in time. What are twelve miles to him, when there is such a feast at the end of it? And then, is he not a Christian? And does he not consider it a joy to be the carrier of such a bundle, with such a loving message, to the aged and feeble Ookoominou? Of course he does.

Others similarly addressed, and charged with loving messages, are rapidly sent off. While the majority of the messengers prefer to make the journey on flying feet, some, perhaps who have bundles for three or four in the same vicinity, prefer to take their fleet dog-trains. It makes but little difference, however, how they go. They are soon all off, and much sooner back again than we inexperienced ones would expect.

Of the great feast itself, it is difficult to give anything like an adequate description. The tables are piled with the various kinds of food, the cups are filled with tea, and all the older people first seated. Some years it was customary for the missionary to have a large table at the head, to which were invited the officials of the Hudson Bay Company and their families, and any visiting friends who might be in the country. The chiefs were also given a place at this table, an honour much appreciated. When all were seated, they very heartily sang as grace before meat, the Cree translation of the Verse:

"Be present at our table, Lord,

Be here and everywhere adored;

These creatures bless, and grant that we

May feast in Paradise with Thee."

When the older people had eaten, the tables were quickly cleared; then again filled and refilled, until all had feasted, and some had even returned "to fill up," as they said, some vacancies discovered. What appetites they had; and what unrestrained enjoyment! No foreboding fears of coming nightmare, or fits of indigestion, disturbed their felicity. Dyspepsia and its kindred ills, had, up to those times, never visited that healthy hunting people; and so, when such a feast of fat things as this was prepared, where they knew they were all welcome guests, they went in for a good time and had it in full measure, without any anxiety for after consequences. It was an epoch in their history—the most blessed day of the year. From it some of them recorded time, as so many moons after the feast; and as the year advanced they made engagements by so many moons before the next feast.

If supplies were still abundant when the last had eaten, the first were set to work again until the bear's ribs were all picked and every haunch of venison had disappeared. Night was grandly closing in, ere this stage in the proceedings was reached. When it did arrive, willing hands soon took down the tables, swept out the building, replaced the seats, lighted the oil lamps, and the intellectual feast was held. For years Mamanowatum, whose familiar name was Big Tom, was appointed chairman. He was a large man, in fact, almost gigantic, slow and deliberate; but he generally made his mark in everything he undertook to do or say. It was amusing to see him in the chair, presiding over a great meeting. He was very much respected by all, and none dared to presume on his apparent good nature. He rose slowly, seeming to get up in short jerks; but when up, he had something to say and said it.

They always opened every kind of a meeting held in the church with religious exercises. Then Mamanowatum made his address, always good and suggestive, the keynote of which was thanksgiving and gratitude to God for the blessings of the year. When he had finished, he called on different Indians for addresses. Some of them were very good also. This is the night of all others, when Indian orators try to be humorous and witty. As a race they do not excel along these lines, but sometimes they get off some very good things. While they began their speeches with some bright pleasantry that brought smiles, and even laughter, there was never anything unbecoming to the place, and all quickly drifted into a strain of thanksgiving to God for his blessings. To listen to their grateful joyous words, one would think they were the most highly favoured people on the earth; that there never was such a feast, such delicious venison, such fat bear meat, such strong tea with so much sugar in it; and that no other people had such kind missionaries. So with more grateful hearts than ever they would sing:

"Praise God from whom all blessings flow."

Thus they talked and rejoiced together in this peculiar service which was all their own. The whites were expected to take back seats on this occasion and say nothing.

About ten o'clock they together sang the doxology; and, with the benediction, pronounced by one of their own number, this most interesting of days, with its varied pleasures and enjoyments, came to a close.

Long years have passed, since with the happy Crees we enjoyed those rich feast days; yet they stand in our missionary life as red-letter days; when our hearts were especially touched by the spontaneous and hearty kindness displayed toward the aged and afflicted ones, who unable to be present, were by the generous gifts sent, made to feel, that they were not forgotten or neglected, but were in a

large measure made partakers of the pleasures of that
eventful day.

Chapter Eight.

The Extra Dog-Train of Supplies, and what came of it.

"As you have so many splendid dogs this winter, why not take an extra train with you, and bring out from Red River some of the food of civilisation, so that we can have it to remind us of other days?"

Thus spake the good wife, who, like myself, sometimes became tired of having the fresh water fish of the country as our principal diet for about one half of the year. During the other six months we lived principally upon game, such as venison, bear's meat, beaver, wild-cat, ptarmigan, rabbits and even muskrats. So, this request to bring out something to eat that savoured of civilisation, was not an unreasonable one. I was going in to Red River settlement on business pertaining to the spiritual advancement of our mission, and this was a good opportunity to bring out with me some things that would add to our comfort and help on in the good work; we had to do so many things for our poor Indians, who were often in trouble, and were constantly looking to us for help.

My splendid dugs obtained from Hamilton, Montreal and elsewhere, had increased and multiplied, until now I had a number of the finest sleigh dogs in the country. When the time came for the long trip, I harnessed them up; and, taking an additional train for the extra supply of food which was suggested by my wife, with my guide and dog drivers, began the journey. In order that we could return with full loads, we started with our sleds loaded with fish, numbers of which we cached at our different camping places, that we might have them on which to feed our dogs on the return journey.

We were several days on the route, as we encountered a fierce blizzard which made travelling with our heavy loads very difficult. However, we reached the settlement, and met with a warm welcome at the home of our friend, the Hon. Mr Sifton. The business that brought us in to civilisation being soon arranged, we began our purchases of supplies for the return, special attention being given to the purchase of the extra load of good things. First, I went to a butcher, and purchased from him about two hundred and fifty pounds of his choicest cuts of meat; telling him, that as it was to be dragged by dogs on a sled some hundreds of miles, I wanted as little bone as possible. He was a decent man and treated me well. Then, I went to a storekeeper, and purchased from him rice, meal, butter, canned vegetables and various other things, making in all, a load of about six hundred pounds. I was very proud of such a load, in addition to the supply of flour which was on the other sleds. Sending my heavily loaded dog-sleds on a couple of days in advance, I followed—in company with Martin Papanekis, a favourite Indian driver—with such dogs as. Voyageur, as leader, and Jack and Cuffy and Caesar behind him, knowing we would have no difficulty in overtaking the rest of our party. We so arranged our return journey, that each night we reached the camp we had used on the outgoing trip. In two places, much to our disgust, we found that the wolves or wolverines, had been too clever for us, and had discovered our cache and devoured our fish. So those nights, we had to feed our dogs from the supplies of meat bought in Red River.

In due time we reached our mission home where there was great satisfaction over the abundance and variety of the supplies secured at such a cost of toil and danger. The bill of fare was much improved, and twice a week we had a little roast of beef or mutton, with vegetables, and a dessert of rice pudding.

For two or three weeks this continued, when our hearts were saddened, and our duties and cares greatly increased, by the breaking out of the measles among our Indians. This epidemic was caused, by the coming in to our country of some free-traders who had lately had the disease. They had been discharged from the hospital as cured; but in some way or other they had carried the germs of the disease so that going in and out of the wigwams they spread the contagion among the natives, and an epidemic broke out. This strange new disease terrified the people.

At that time I had parties of Indians at Oomeme River, and also at Berens River, where we were then living. About this same time the measles also broke out among a number of pagan Indians under the rule of Thickfoot, a stubborn yet friendly old chief who refused to become a Christian. At this place we had but lately completed a mission house, some outbuildings, and a comfortable school-house, which we were using as a church until the latter should be completed. All the timber for these buildings we had drawn with our dogs from a large island several miles out from, the mainland. When the measles broke out, and we saw the fear of the Indians, at once, as far as possible, we turned our mission premises into a hospital. In addition to the buildings already mentioned, we also put up for the sick our large buffalo leather tent. Here, on improvised beds and couches, we gathered about us the afflicted ones, making them as comfortable as our limited means would allow.

Over at Oomeme River, our Christian Indians fortunately escaped; but the pagan Indians, among whom the disease broke out, were wild with fear, and in many cases acted in a manner to aggravate the disease. Some of them, when they broke out, rushed from their heated wigwams and rolled themselves in the snow, which of course was most disastrous treatment, resulting in the death of numbers. Thereupon, their relatives became so terrified, that, being afraid to bury their bodies, they stripped the wigwams from around them, leaving them exposed to the devouring wolves; and then, sent word over to me, that if I desired their friends to be decently buried, I must come over and do it myself. Hearing this, I took some boards, nails, hammer, spades and other things necessary, and with some Indians, hurried over to the place. After some persuasion, I succeeded in getting an Indian family to move their wigwam from the spot where it had stood the whole winter, and where constantly the fire had been burning; and there, where the ground was yet warm and unfrozen, dug the grave, making it sufficiently large for all who had died. With our boards we made the coffins, and after a simple religious service buried their dead.

At Berens River, our method of procedure among our sick was something like this. Early in the morning, large pots partly filled with water were hung over a good fire. Into them were put several pounds of the good fresh beef or mutton which we had brought from civilisation. When well boiled, several pounds of rice were stirred in and the whole left to boil until cooked into a rich nourishing soup. Then nourishing flat cakes were made in abundance. While this breakfast for the sick was being prepared, the missionary, with his assistants, was busily engaged in making the rounds of the sick. Their various wants were attended to, medicine was given, and every thing that could be, was cheerfully done for their comfort. Then, the missionary's wife, with her helpers, followed with kettles of warm soup, bread and tea. Meals of this nourishing food were given to, and much relished by, the afflicted ones. There were some such severe cases, that at times it looked as though it would be impossible to save them; but with heaven's blessing on our efforts, we were successful in bringing about the recovery of every case under our immediate care. While doing everything that we could for their physical recovery, we had grand opportunities for imparting religious instruction. Sweet hymns, translated into their own language, were sung, and the exceeding great and precious promises of the blessed Book, were often read and explained at every bedside. Their fear of this strange new disease left them, and they became patient and hopeful. The result was, that while among the pagan Indians at Oomeme River there were many deaths, not one of our Christian Indians died.

When the last case was cured and the disease had disappeared, we took stock of our supplies. We found that all of that extra dog-train of food, together with a large quantity of flour and other things, had been used up in feeding our poor sick people. Not one-tenth of the whole had come to our own table; and so we had once again to fall back upon our native food. Fish was again our diet twenty-one times a week. But, we had the great joy and satisfaction of knowing that, in all human probability, we had saved the lives of many of our people; and had found such a place in their hearts, that our future efforts to evangelise or to help along in the blessed life, would be very much more effective.

## Chapter Nine.

## A Lesson never to be Forgotten.

When I was a small boy, my father was stationed on a large mission in the back woods of Canada. The hardy emigrants from the Old World were crowding into that new country, and every year additional thousands of acres of grain were growing, where shortly before the dark primeval forests, which had stood for centuries, held possession.

The native Indian tribes were retreating before this irresistible march of the white man, or were settling on reservations selected for them by the government. For years they retained their right to roam about, and kill the game which still abounded, but which was rapidly becoming less as the white settlements increased. In addition to their hunting and fishing, the industrious Indians added to their comfort by manufacturing native baskets, brooms, handles for axes, hoes and similar articles, which they sold to the friendly settlers for food and clothing. Those that left the fire-water alone, and were industrious, were thus able to live comfortably.

To these Indians on their reservations the Gospel was proclaimed by the self-sacrificing missionaries, as they travelled their toilsome rounds. These visits were not made in vain. Many of these children of the forest, sick and dissatisfied with their old paganism which gave no peace to their troubled spirits, gladly received the truth, and became earnest, consistent Christians. Their godly lives were, in many places, a constant reproof to the inconsistencies and sins of their white neighbours. At rare intervals in my boyhood days it was my great privilege to be permitted to

accompany my father to some of the Indian encampments
that were not very far from our home, I well remember the
sweet plaintive voices of the Indians, as they sung some of
our hymns which had been translated into their language.
Their devout and attentive demeanour during the religious
services, deeply impressed me. It was ever a great pleasure
to visit them in their wigwams, to see the young people at
their sports, and the older ones at their work: building
canoes, or making baskets.

In my boyish curiosity, I did not confine my rambling
solely to the Christian Indians; but, as all were very
friendly, I wandered about the encampments to the
different wigwams, to see what I could that was novel and
interesting. Being known as the son of the Blackcoat—for
in this way was the missionary designated by the tribe—I
was always welcomed in the wigwams, and was given a
seat in the circle around the fire.

In one wigwam the following characteristic incident
occurred which made a deep impression on my mind.
Seated on the ground were representatives of three
generations, all, except the aged grandfather, busily
engaged in work, principally basket-making. He was a
patriarchal-looking old man, and, to my youthful eyes as he
sat there on his blanket smoking his long pipe, seemed to
be absorbed in thought, noticing neither me nor any one
else.

The youngest of the company, and the one that naturally
attracted my attention, was a young lad of about my own
age. He was busily engaged with an Indian crooked knife,
endeavouring to make an arrow. In his eagerness to
succeed, he let his knife slip, and unfortunately, cut himself
very badly. At the sight of the blood,—which flowed

freely, for the wound was an ugly one—the lad set up a
howl of pain and alarm, which greatly startled his stoical
relatives. Relief was quickly afforded, the cut covered with
balsam and tied up in a piece of deer skin. Not one word of
sympathy did the boy receive; but on the contrary from
nearly all in the wigwam arose a chorus of indignation and
disgust. To them it was a great disgrace that one of their
family, and he a boy of so many winters, should howl and
cry like that, for such a trifling injury.

How the other families would laugh at them when they
heard of it! It looked for a time as if they would severely
punish him, not for his awkwardness in handling his knife,
but because he did not control his feelings and treat the
wound and the pain with utter indifference.

The old grandfather especially, was deeply stirred and
indignant at conduct so unworthy of his grandson, to whom
evidently he was deeply attached.

Indians very seldom punish their children. Upon the boys
especially, the rod is seldom used. The girls in the heathen
families often have a hard time of it, being frequently
knocked about and beaten; but the boys generally escape,
even if they richly deserve punishment. Here, however, was
a very serious case. The boy had committed a crime in
crying out at an ordinary cut on his hand, inflicted by
himself. It would never do to let this pass. The lad must be
taught a lesson he would never forget. And this is the way
in which it was done, much to my amazement, by his old
grandfather.

Placing near him the lad, who evidently was now feeling
that he had been very guilty, he gave him a talk upon the
duty of bearing pain without uttering a cry, or even a groan.

Then the old man, who had been a great warrior in his younger days, told him, that unless he were more courageous than that, he would never become a brave warrior or a good hunter; and, that unless he was able to control his feelings, and never cry out no matter what happened, they could never respect him any more than they would an old grandmother.

While the old man talked excitedly to him, now thoroughly roused out of his usual calm demeanour, he renewed the fire which had partly burnt down. When, by the addition of some very dry wood, it was burning very vigorously, he again turned quickly to his grandson, and speaking out sharply and excitedly, said: "See here! Look at me! This is the way a brave warrior should stand pain!" Then, to my horror, he suddenly reached out his hand, and holding one finger in the flame, kept it there until it was fearfully burnt.

During this sickening ordeal, not a muscle of the old man's face quivered; not a groan escaped from his firmly set lips. To judge from his appearance, it might have been a stick that he was burning. When at length he drew back the crisp burnt finger of his now blistered hand, he held it toward his grandson and gave him another lecture, telling him among other things that if he ever expected to be great or honoured among his people, he must hear pain without flinching or uttering a cry.

## Chapter Ten.

### The Honest Indian; or, Venison for Pemmican.

Years ago the missionaries living in the northern part of what were then known as the Hudson Bay territories, were often so remote from civilisation, that they were obliged to depend principally on fish and game for their livelihood. Hence, in times of scarcity, they welcomed the arrival of a hunter who came in with plenty of game.

One cold wintry day, a man of this description made his appearance at our mission home. He was a fine stalwart Indian, and, in the quiet way of his people, came into our kitchen without knocking. Unstrapping from his back a fine haunch of venison, he threw it down upon the table. As our supplies of food were very limited at the time—for we were averaging hardly more than two good meals a day—I was glad to see this welcome addition; and so, after I had cordially greeted him, I said:

"What shall I give you for this venison?"

"I want nothing for it, as it belongs to you," was his answer.

"You must be mistaken," I replied, "as I never saw you before, and have had no dealings with you."

"Oh, but it does belong to you, and I want nothing more for it," he insisted.

"Excuse me," I said, "but you must let me pay you for it. We are very glad to get it, as there is little food in the house; but we have a rule here, that we pay the Indians for everything we get from them."

The reason we had come to this determination, was because we had found by rather dear experience,—as we presume other missionaries on similar fields have,—that the natives have an idea the missionary is rich, or that he is backed up by wealthy churches; and, with unlimited resources at his disposal, is able to make large gifts in return for lesser ones received. A few rabbits, or a brace of ducks would be given with great politeness to the missionary or his wife. Then the donor, often accompanied by his wife and several children, would remain to dinner, and, in all probability, eat the greater part of the gift. Of course they must be asked to supper—and they had glorious appetites. As they still lingered on until time for retiring arrived, the missionary was at length obliged to hint, that he thought they would better go and see if their wigwam was where they left it in the morning. This would generally bring things to a crisis, and the man would say: "Ever since we came we have only been waiting to get the present you are going to give us for the one we gave you."

While they were contented to sell at a reasonable rate the various things which they could supply for our needs, yet, if a present were accepted, they expected something many times its value. Had this been allowed to continue, we would have been speedily left destitute of everything in the house. Therefore, not many weeks before the arrival of this strange Indian with the venison, as a precautionary measure we had made a rule that no more presents were to be received from the Indians; but that for everything brought which we needed, such as meat, fish, or moccasins, there was to be a fair tariff price mutually agreed upon. Yet in spite of all this, here was a stalwart Indian insisting, that I should receive a haunch of venison without payment. Judging from some past experiences, I was fearful that if I accepted it as a present, it would about bankrupt me. So I again said to him:

"You must let me pay you for this."

"No, no," he energetically replied. "I take no pay. It belongs to you."

"How do you make that out?" I inquired, more perplexed than ever.

Then he proceeded to give me his explanation, which deeply interested me, and which will also I am sure interest my readers.

First, he began by asking me a few questions:

"Did you make a trip with your guide and dog drivers to Burntwood River last winter?"

"Yes, I did," was my answer.

"And were your dog-sleds not heavily loaded?"

"Yes," I replied.

"And was there not a heavy fall of snow followed by a blizzard, which as you had no trail through the deep snow, made it very difficult travelling?"

"Quite true," I replied, for all had happened just as he was describing it. "And did you not at a certain place make a cache of some of your pemmican and other heavy things, so as to lighten your loads, that your dogs might make better time?"

"Yes," I answered, for well did I remember that long journey, and the fearful storm which made travelling through the trackless forest almost impossible.

I had gone on a journey of several hundreds of miles to carry the Gospel to some Indians who were still in the darkness of paganism. I travelled with sixteen dogs and four Indian companions, and there was not the least vestige of a road. This is the one great drawback; and any party of hunters, traders, or missionaries, wishing to travel with any rapidity, must send one of their number on ahead of the dog trains to mark out the path with his great snow shoes as he strides along. The skill and endurance with which this work is performed, is marvellous and almost incredible to those who have not witnessed it. Often the country for days together is tamely monotonous, without any striking feature in the landscape, and without the least sign of human footsteps. Clouds may gather and cover the whole heavens with a sombre grey mantle, so that the white man gets bewildered and does not know south from north, or east from west. Yet the Indian guide pushes on without hesitancy, and with unerring accuracy.

While endeavouring to push on as rapidly as possible, we were assailed by a fierce storm. The snowfall was so great, that, with our heavy loads, speedy progress was an utter impossibility. We found, that we must either lighten our loads, or be content to lose much valuable time on the way. After talking it over with my Indians, we decided on the former course, and so, a "cache" was made. A number of the heavier articles were tied up in large blankets, some saplings bent down by the stalwart men, and the bundles fastened in their tops. When let go, the young trees sprang up, and thus held their loads so far above the ground that they were safe from the prowling wolves or wolverines. This plan is very much safer than that of using large trees, as up the latter many of the wild animals can climb, and short work would be made of the "cache."

With lightened sleds—although some of the things left behind were sadly missed—we hurried on, and after a few days reached our destination. We found the majority of the Indians glad to see us, and anxious for instruction in the ways of the great Book. They had become dissatisfied with the ways of their fathers, and had lost all faith in their conjurers, so they listened with great attention to what we had to tell of the Gospel of the Son of God.

While we were thus engaged in our missionary duties, blizzards were raging through that cold northland; so that when we began the long home journey, we discovered but few traces of the trail, which our snow shoes and dog-trains had made not very long before. However, my guide was very clever, and my splendid dogs most sagacious, so we travelled home most of the way on the same route, even though the original path was deeply buried by the snow.

The place where our cache had been made was duly reached; and glad enough were we to obtain the additional supplies it contained, for we had been on short allowance for some time. The strong arms of my Indians soon bent down the saplings, untied the bundles and consigned them to the different dog-sleds. To my surprise, I observed, that at one of the bundles—the heaviest article in which had been a piece of pemmican weighing perhaps fifty or sixty pounds—my men were talking and gesticulating most earnestly. In answer to my inquiries, they said, that that bundle had been taken down during our absence, and a piece of pemmican had been cut off and taken away.

"Nonsense!" I replied. "You are surely mistaken. It looks to me just as it was when we put it up. And then there was not the vestige of a track here when we returned."

However, in spite of my protestations, my men were confident that some pemmican had been taken by a stranger, and that the blizzard had covered up the tracks. With a little more discussion the matter was dropped, and after a good meal we proceeded on our way.

Months later, along came this strange Indian with the venison and his story, which we will now let him finish:

"I was out hunting in those forests through which you passed: for they are my hunting grounds. I found the trail of a moose, and for a long time I followed it up, but did not succeed in getting a shot. I had poor success on that hunting trip. Shooting nothing for some days, I became very hungry. While pushing along through the woods, I came across your trail and saw your cache. So when I saw it was the missionary's cache, the friend of the Indian, I was glad, and I said to myself. If he were here, and knew that I was hungry, he would say: 'Help yourself:'—and that was just what I did. I pulled down a sapling, and opening the bundle, cut off a piece of pemmican—just enough to make me feel comfortable under my belt until I could reach my wigwam, far away. Then I tied up the bundle, fastened it in the treetop, and let it swing up again. And now I have brought you this venison, to pay for that pemmican which I took."

Honest man! He had carried the haunch of venison on his
back, a distance of about sixty miles.

Of course I was delighted, and while complimenting him
for his honesty, inquired how he knew that it was my party
that had made the cache, rather than a party of Indian
hunters.

Without any hesitancy he replied: "Oh I saw your snow
shoe tracks in the snow."

"Impossible!" I answered; "for the snow shoes used by the
whole party were made by Sandy, my Indian boy, and were
all of one pattern."

"That no matter," he answered, while his eyes twinkled
with amusement. "Snow shoes all right, but I saw your
tracks all the time. When Indian walk, he walk with toes in;
when white man walk, he walk with toes out. So I saw
where the missionary make tracks all the time."

We all voted him a clever, as well as an honest Indian, and
rejoiced that under the faithful teachings of another
missionary, this red Indian of the forest, had been so
grounded in the lessons of the sermon on the mount.

Chapter Eleven.

The Vindication of the Sabbath.

When the missionaries go among the heathen preaching the blessed Gospel of the great Book, they necessarily have to begin, with first principles. When good impressions have been made, and hearts touched, then follows religious instruction in matters of which they have been perfectly ignorant! and much that is false, and often very childish, has to be unlearned.

To these people, before the arrival of the missionary, the Sabbath was utterly unknown. The preaching of it at first filled them with perplexity and trouble. They thought that it would interfere with their plans, and so break up their hunting arrangements as to bring them to absolute want. They were poor, even though working and fishing every day; and to give up one day out of every seven, and not fire a gun, or set a net—what would become of them! Thus argued some of the Indians.

Faithfully and lovingly the missionaries set before them the commands of God adding the promises of blessings to the obedient. The Book itself was diligently searched, and there was a great desire to know, if such passages as the one we here quote referred to white people and Indians now: "If thou turn away thy foot from the Sabbath, from doing thy pleasure on my holy day, and call the Sabbath a delight, the holy of the Lord, honourable: and shalt honour him not doing thine own ways, nor finding thine own pleasure, nor speaking thine own words, then shalt thou delight thyself in the Lord, and I will cause thee to ride upon the high places of the earth, and feed thee with the heritage of Jacob thy father; for the mouth of the Lord hath spoken it."

At last, under faithful teaching, aided by the blessed Spirit, the Christian Indians resolved to take the Book for their guide, and to keep the Sabbath day. At once, the guns and bows and arrows were put aside, and the fish-nets were left hanging in the breeze for that day. No traps were visited, neither were the axes lifted up against the trees. Their simple meals were cooked and eaten, and all who could attend, were found in the house of God three times each Sabbath.

But now arose fierce opposition from an unexpected quarter. The great fur-trading company that had for so long a time held despotic power in the land, in their short-sightedness,—fearing a diminution in the returns of the fur by the hunters if one-seventh of the time was to be, as they put it, spent in idleness,—sneered at the actions of the missionaries, and by bribes and threats, endeavoured to induce the Indians to ignore their teachings on the subject.

When, the summer tripping began, and the Indians refused to travel or work in the boats on the Sabbath, the action of the company developed into downright persecution. Some description of this "tripping" in that great wild northland is necessary, in order that our readers may understand the position taken by the Sabbath-keeping Indians, and its most satisfactory results.

So remote from the seaboard are some of the interior posts of the Hudson Bay Company, that seven years, and sometimes more elapsed, ere the furs obtained for the goods sent, could reach the London market. The bales of goods were first shipped by the company's vessels to York factory, on the Hudson Bay. Then they were taken by the Indian trippers in strong boats that would hold from three to five tons. A number of these boats constituted a "brigade." A captain of the whole was appointed, and a good state of discipline maintained.

The first brigade would take the bales up the rivers, often having to pass many dangerous places and encounter many risks. Great care and watchfulness were necessary, and yet in spite of all, boats were sometimes wrecked and lives lost. The hardest part of the work was in what was called, "making the portages." Some of the rivers are full of falls and rapids that are impassable for the boats. Here the portages have to be made. The hardy boatmen row up to the rapids as close as is safe, unload their cargoes, and carry them on their backs to the selected spot below the obstruction in the river. Then the boats have to be hauled ashore, and dragged overland by the united strength of the several crews to the same place; here they are again launched, and with cargoes aboard, the journey is resumed. On some of these trips the number of portages runs up into the scores. Great lakes have to be crossed where fierce storms at times rage, and where head-winds blow with such fury, that sometimes the brigades are delayed many days.

At Norway house,—which for many years was the great northern depôt for the company's goods, and the great distributing centre for the interior parts,—this first brigade would exchange its cargo of goods for the bales of rich furs which another brigade, that had come from the further interior, perhaps from Athabasca or the Saskatchewan country, had brought down thus far on their way to the ships for the London market. Then this second brigade would return hundreds of miles into the interior; and, meeting another brigade from regions still more remote, would exchange its cargo of goods with this third brigade, for regions yet more distant. Thus it would go on, until some of the bales of goods were more than three thousand miles from the seaboard where they were landed; and the different posts had their supply of goods for the fur trade with the Indians. So it happened, that years elapsed ere the goods reached some of the places; and the furs also were years in reaching the ship for England.

All of this heavy work was performed by the Indian boatmen, or "trippers," as they were called. They were the fur-hunters during the cold winter months; but so long as there was open water—that is, no ice—they were employed by hundreds to take in goods and bring out furs.

The one despotic command delivered to these brigades by the company was, "push on!" They argued: The summer in these high latitudes is short; we must make the most of it. Every day tells, and there must be no lagging by the way. The result was, that the men were worked to the last degree of endurance. Many failed at the oar, while others dropped under the heavy loads on the difficult portages. "Fill up the ranks quickly, and push on," was the order. It was all excitement, and rush, and high pressure, from the beginning of the tripping season until the close. There was no relaxation—no Sabbath—no rest.

It seemed utter folly for the missionary to come in where such a condition of things existed, and say to the best men of the best brigade: "We know the summer is short, and it is essential for the welfare of the company and your own wages, that the goods should be taken in, and the furs brought out. But a Higher Power has said, 'Remember the Sabbath day to keep it holy, so when Saturday night overtakes you, tie up your boats, lay aside your oars, and rest in quietness and devotion until God's day is over.'"

The company in their blindness were at first astounded, then enraged. To lose one-seventh of the short summer, when, as it was, the brigades were sometimes caught by the ice, would never do! This fanaticism must be stopped! They threatened—they persecuted the missionary and the Indians. Their monopoly in the country gave them great power, and they wielded it unmercifully. Unable to induce the missionary by bribes or threats to take another stand, they resorted to persecution; and by calumnies most foul, strove to destroy his good name, and to drive him out of the country.

He was a wise and judicious, as well as a brave man; and, standing at his post, endeavoured to show his rich and powerful detractors, that no harm would come to them by their employees resting one day in seven. He bravely declared, that a man could do more work in six days by resting the seventh, than by working continuously; and he challenged them to the test.

At first the statement, which had been, so conclusively proved to be true was laughed to scorn. However, as the missionary and his Christian Indians remained true, the company were obliged to yield so far as to send off a Sabbath-keeping brigade, which they did with many fears and misgivings. To their surprise, they did their work just as well, and returned in less time, with the men in better health than those who knew no Sabbath. The logic of actual success triumphed eventually. All opposition ceased, and up to the time when the old order of things came to an end, and oars gave way to steam power, no one was found rash

enough to question the ability of the Sabbath-keeping
Indians to excel in work those who kept not the day of rest.

I often travelled with those Christian Indians, and the
Sabbaths spent on these long trips, are sweet and happy
memories. Up to the last hour on Saturday when it was safe
to travel, the journey would be pursued, until, in some quiet
harbour or cosy bend in the river, safe from sudden storms
or tornadoes, the boats would be securely fastened, and the
cargoes carefully covered with the oilcloths. After a supper
cooked on the rocks, all would gather around the bright
camp-fire for the evening devotions. A hymn would be
sung, a chapter of the good Book read, and prayer offered
by one or two of the company. The Sabbath would be spent
quietly and restfully, with at least two impressive and
simple services. On Monday, at first blush of morn, we
were up, and, after a hasty meal and a prayer, the journey
would be resumed with renewed vigour.

Thus was the Sabbath introduced among the northern
Indians.

Chapter Twelve.

God more Powerful than the Conjurer.

The following beautiful story deserves a place among the very many real answers to prayer. Still does the Lord say to his followers: "I will yet for this be inquired of by the house of Israel, to do it for them."

Our Indian converts believe in God. With a simple, childlike faith they take Him at his word. One of our Indians at his baptism, received the English name of Edmund Stephenson. He was an earnest, simple Christian. His religion made him industrious, and so by his diligent hunting and fishing he provided comfortably for his wife and two little ones.

One evening, about the middle of last October, he left his family at his little home at Norway House, and started up a rapid river to visit some of his relatives, who lived several miles away. In those high latitudes the cold winter sets in so early that already the river, was covered with ice. To make the trip much quicker he fastened on his skates, and when last seen, was speeding rapidly away in the evening twilight.

He did not return the next day as he had promised, and his family becoming alarmed, sent an Indian messenger to inquire the reason. To his surprise he was informed by the friends that Edmund had not visited them and they knew not of his whereabouts. When these tidings were carried home there was great alarm, and a search party was quickly organised. From the point where he was last seen alive, they carefully examined the ice, and, after a little time, discovered the most conclusive evidence that the poor man was drowned.

Over a part of the river where the current is very rapid, they discovered that the ice had been broken through; and although all was now again firmly frozen over, yet, in the congealed mass, they discovered one of Edmund's deer-skin gloves, a button of his coat, and other evidences that he had here fallen through the ice, and had made a most desperate effort to escape. As it was nearly dark when the searchers made these discoveries as to the place and manner, of his death, they were obliged to be satisfied with this, and to postpone the search for the body until the next day.

Early the next morning they set to work diligently. As much snow had fallen since the previous evening, they were very much hampered in their efforts; and, although a large number of men, with snow shovels, axes and grappling irons sought carefully in many places for the remains, several days passed, and they were still unsuccessful in their efforts.

Among the searchers were some Indians who still believed in the skill and supernatural powers of the conjurers, or medicine men. These, having become discouraged in their efforts, resolved to consult one of these old men, so they said:

"Let us go and consult old Kwaskacarpo, and get him to conjure for us, and tell us where to find the body."

The Christian Indians protested against this, and tried to dissuade them; but to no purpose they were so discouraged in their efforts. So they carried gifts of tea and tobacco to the conjurer, and told him of the object of their coming. In response to their wishes, and in return for their gifts, he took his sacred drum and medicine-bag into the tent, drummed away noisily until he worked himself up into a kind of frenzy or delirium, and then told them where to cut the ice and drag for the body of their dead comrade.

When the Christian Indians heard that these others had gone to the conjurer for help, they were very much grieved. One especially, a grand old man by the name of Thomas Mustagan, was very much depressed in spirit. While feeling deeply the loss of Edmund, he was very much hurt when the news reached him, that some of the searchers instead of going to God in their perplexity and trouble, had, like King Saul, resorted to such disputable agencies.

No sooner had he received this news, than he resolved to adopt a very different course. Getting his wife to cook a quantity of food; he carried it, with some kettles of tea, to a spot on the shore near to where the men were diligently searching for the body.

Clearing away the snow he made a fire; and, when the tea was prepared, called the hungry and almost discouraged men around him, and made them eat his food and drink his tea. Then he talked to them of the one living and true God, and of His power to hear and answer prayer. He spoke of the foolishness and wickedness of those, who, having heard about Him, had gone and consulted the wicked old conjurer. "Let us go to that God about whom we have been taught by our missionaries. He is the one to help us in our trouble."

With the people all around him, he kneeled down in snow, and earnestly and reverently asked God to hear and help them in their sorrow and perplexity. He prayed that wisdom might be given them, so that they might find the body of their dear friend lying somewhere in that cold river; that they might take it up, and bury it in their little village graveyard. He asked God very earnestly to comfort the poor sorrowing widow and the little helpless children. Thus with believing faith did this venerable old Indian of more than fourscore winters, call upon God.

When they arose from their knees he said: "Now trusting in God to answer us, let us go to work."

On account of the quantity of snow that had fallen on the ice, they had first to scrape it away, and then use their judgment about where to cut through the ice, and drag for the body. Although Thomas was so old a man, he now seemed the most alert and active of the party. By common consent, he was given charge of the party of Christian Indians, who now worked diligently under his direction.

In the meantime, the old conjurer Kwaskacarpo in a confident voice told his followers, that he had conjured, and the answer was, that they were to cut the ice in a certain designated place.

Paying no attention to him or his party, the Christian Indians worked away, and as fast as the ice was cleared of snow, Thomas looked through as well as he could.

All at once he arose quickly from a spot of semi-transparent ice which he had been carefully examining, and calling to the men with the axes and ice-chisels, he said:

"Try here."

Soon they had a large hole cut, the grappling irons were brought into use, and there hundreds of yards from the place where the conjurer had directed his followers to look for it, the body was found.

Thomas, while intently searching through the ice, had seen on the under surface at that place a quantity of air bubbles. The thought came to him, that here the body had rested, and the last air from the lungs had escaped and formed these bubbles. He had asked for wisdom and divine direction and he was not disappointed, for in less than an hour after these pious Indians had been on their knees in earnest prayer the body of their comrade was being borne away to his home, and from thence to its final resting place in the "God's Acre" of the little Christian village.

## Chapter Thirteen.

### Betsy, the Indian Wife.

She was not a bad looking woman, but she had such a sorrowful face that never seemed to have on it a smile. Mrs Young and I had both noticed this, and had spoken to each other about it. Her name was Betsy. She was the wife of an Indian whose name was Atenou, but who, when baptised, had, like most of his countrymen, asked for the addition to it of an English name, and so was known as Robert Atenou. His record seemed to be that of a quiet, industrious sort of an Indian, who fished and hunted as did the rest, and gave trouble to none. As he, like many of his people, was gifted with readiness of utterance, and was very faithful in his attendance at all of the religious services, and seemed to be living a godly life, he had been, given an official position in the church, which, he very much appreciated.

It was noticed however, that Robert's advancement in the church, did not seem to remove the cloud that was on his wife's face. While the other women were so bright and happy and thankful at the change which Christianity had brought into their lives, and were at times not slow in speaking about it, she was a very marked exception.

Not wishing to pry into her affairs, while perplexed, we were obliged for a time to remain in the dark, and could only conjecture as to the cause.

Perhaps the most marvellous and conspicuous evidence of the blessedness of the Gospel, next to its divine power in the salvation of the soul, is to be seen in the glorious way in which it uplifts women. Sad indeed is the condition of

women in lands unreached by the blessed influences of
Christianity. He whose wonderful and tender love for His
mother, and for the goodly women who ministered to Him,
was so manifested when He walked this earth of ours, is
Jesus still. And wherever His name is successfully
proclaimed, and hearts opened to receive Him, there at
once is a glorious uplifting of woman from a condition of
inferiority and degradation, into one where she is honoured
and respected.

The northern Indian tribes on this continent, while not very
warlike, or much in the habit of going after the scalps of
their enemies, had other crimes and sins, which showed
that they were fallen and sinful, and much in need of the
Gospel. Among the defects and wickednesses of the men,
was the almost universal contempt for, and cruelty to the
women. If a man spoke or acted kindly to his wife, or
mother, or daughter, it was by them considered a sign of
weakness and effeminacy. To be harsh and cold toward the
women, was supposed to be one of the signs of the ideal
Indian toward which they were ever striving. All manual
labour, apart from hunting and fishing, was considered
degrading to be left to the women, and some, as much as
possible, even left the fishing to them. Where there were no
tribal wars, the perfect Indian was only the great hunter.
And with the great hunter, his work ended when the game
was killed. If it were at all possible to send his wife or
mother to the spot where the animal lay, that his arrow or
gun had brought down, he would scorn to carry or drag it
back to camp. He had killed the bear, or moose, or reindeer,
or whatever animal it might happen to be, and now it was
woman's work to take it to the wigwam, and as quickly as
possible prepare for him his meal. Thus we have seen the
great stalwart six-footed hunter come stalking into the
village with his gun upon his shoulder, while the poor

mother, or wife, or daughter, came trudging on behind, almost crushed down with the weight of the game upon her back. He carried the gun—she the game.

Then, no matter how tired she might be with the heavy burden, no time was allowed for rest. With a quick harsh "kinipe" (hurry); she was soon at work. The skin was quickly and skilfully removed, and some of the savoury meat was cooked and placed before her husband or son. Not a mouthful would she be allowed to taste until the despot had leisurely finished, unless it were to pick some of the bones which he condescendingly threw to her, as, at a distance from him, she sat with the girls and dogs. Thus she was treated as a slave, or drudge, or beast of burden. Then when sickness or old age came on, and she became unable to work and toil and slave, she was without mercy put out of existence: the usual method being strangulation.

This was the sad condition of women in various parts of this great continent ere the Gospel reached the Indian tribes. Very marvellous and striking have been the transformations which we have witnessed among those to whom we had gone with the truth. At some places we witnessed changes wrought by the labours of the worthy men who had preceded us; in other places we were permitted both to sow the seed and see the glorious harvest.

Although, from the white man's standpoint the people here were poor, yet the little houses, where were the followers of the Lord Jesus, were homes of happiness, and the spirit of kindliness and affection everywhere prevailed. There men and women lived on terms of equality. No longer did the men eat alone and of the best of the game and fish, but all together men and women, boys and girls as one loving family, shared proportionately what had been secured. The result was, there was a spirit of contentment and happiness in our mission village that was very gratifying.

However, amidst these happy faces and notes of thanksgiving, here was this one sorrowful face and silent tongue. What was the cause? The truth came out at last, and in a way that was almost dramatic.

Mrs Young and I were busy one day with our routine duties, when Betsy came into our home, and hardly taking time enough to give the usual morning salutation exclaimed in a most decided way; "Robert is not kind to me, and does not treat me like the other men, who profess to be Christians, treat their wives."

This strong emphatic remark startled us, and at once gave us the clue to the cause of the sorrowful face. At first we hardly knew just how to answer such an emphatic utterance, and so in silence waited for her to proceed. But there she sat quietly her face nearly hidden in her black shawl, seeming to be afraid to proceed further. So we had at length to break the awkward silence, by saying we were very sorry to hear her words and could not understand their meaning, as Robert seemed to be a very good man, and an earnest Christian.

This at once caused her to break her silence, and turning around to me, she said:

"Yes, that is it. If he did not so profess to be a Christian, I would never mind it, and would silently bear it; but he professes to be a Christian, and does not treat me in the way in which the other Christian men treat their wives."

Then she quieted down, and in a very straightforward way told us her story, which was as follows:

"When Robert goes out and shoots a deer, it is true he does not come home with the gun upon his shoulder, and make me go out on his trail and bring in the game; he brings it in himself, like the other Christian Indians; but when it is brought in, he makes me skin it; and then takes the two haunches over to the fort, and there exchanges them with the fur-traders for some flour, tea and sugar, which he brings home. I have to cook for him a fore-shoulder of the deer, make cakes at the fire, out of his flour, and then when the tea is made and supper is ready, sit and watch him, and our boys, and any men visitors who happen to be there— and a number are generally around by that time—eat until all is consumed. He never gives any of these good things to me, or to the girls. We have to go out in a canoe, and, with a net, catch some fish for our food. And yet," she added, with some bitterness, "he calls himself a Christian; and treats us in this way, as though he had never heard the missionary."

Of course we were both indignant as she told her story, and were not slow in letting her know of our annoyance at her having been, so treated. But wife-like, and woman-like, when I said:

"Robert shall hear of this, and shall be straightened out forthwith," her fears were aroused, and it seemed as though she were now frightened at what she had said. However there was not much difficulty in quieting her fears, although at first it did seem as though she would rush out of the house, and return to her tent, and submit to the humiliating life which she saw should not have continued so long.

After a little consultation with Mrs Young, our course of action was agreed upon. It was, that Betsy should be kept at the mission house until I had assembled in the church a number of the elderly Christian men; and later Robert, whom we learned from his wife was then at his tent, was to be summoned.

But little time was required in which to gather the men I wanted, as most of the people were then at their homes. They were completely in the dark as to the object for which I had called them together. When in the church. I sent for Mrs Young and Betsy to join us. Poor Betsy was now so frightened, that it seemed as if, like a startled deer, she would run to the woods. However, she was in good hands. Mrs Young spoke soothing words, and cheered her much by telling her, that what she had done in coming to us with the story of her wrongs was perfectly right, and that very soon every thing would be cleared up.

Shortly after the two women came in and took seats together, Robert, for whom I had sent two men, walked in.

At first he was much surprised at the gathering, and especially puzzled and perplexed at seeing his wife sitting there by the side of the wife of the missionary. Before he could say anything, I pointed out a seat for him where he would be in full view of his brother Indians, and yet, where his presence would not overawe, or crush down his wife. Soon after, I locked the church door and said:

"Let us pray."

After prayers I turned to Betsy, and said:

"Now Betsy, if what you told Mrs Young and me in the mission house is true, and I believe it is, I want you now to tell the story over again that these Christian men may hear it. Never mind the fact of Robert's being here; if he is a Christian, as he says he is, the hearing of it will, I hope, do him good."

The faces of those Indians were studies. None knew, not even Robert himself, what Betsy had to say; and so they waited in amazement to hear her story.

With an encouraging word from Mrs Young, she began; and although at first she was timid and nervous, she soon recovered her self-possession, and in a perfectly natural manner told the story of the treatment she and the girls had received from the hands of her husband. With renewed emphasis she dwelt on that which seemed to have given her the most sorrow? "If he had not so professed to be a Christian, I would not have so much minded it."

Indians are the best listeners in the world. They never interrupt anyone in his talk. And so, even Robert, who at first was simply dumbfounded and amazed, controlled himself and held his peace. Very few white men could have done so. I had purposely so placed him, that if he had suddenly attempted violence, stronger men could instantly have restrained him. But nothing of the kind was attempted. As his wife went on and on, showing the difference between his conduct toward her and their girls, and that of the other Christian men toward their wives and daughters, Robert's head went lower and lower, until there he sat, humiliated and disgraced before his brethren. When Betsy finished her talk and sat down, I turned to the good men there assembled and merely said:

"What do you think of such conduct on the part of one who professes to be a Christian?"

Their indignation knew no bounds. Indian like, they had let Betsy tell her whole story without any interruption; but the looks on their faces as she proceeded, told how deeply affected they were. Now that they had heard her story, it seemed as though they all wanted to speak at ones; but there are well understood, although unwritten, rules of precedence among them, so the first in order spoke, and then the second, and then the third, and so on.

How they did dress the poor fellow down! While it was very severe, it was Christian and brotherly. They spoke as men who were grieved and wounded.

"Is this the way you have acted! You, Robert Atenou, who for so long a time have professed to be a Christian; you, to treat your poor wife and children like that; as though no Bible, or missionary had come among us! Now we know why Betsy has been so sad, and did not rejoice like the other women."

Thus they faithfully chided him, and expressed their sorrow at his heartless conduct.

Poor Robert, I had soon to pity him. First, of course, I was a little anxious as to the way in which a once proud-spirited fiery Indian, would take his wife's arraignment of his misdoings and selfishness, and also these reprimands from his brethren. However, it turned out all right. Robert just buried his bronzed face in his hands, and received it all in silence. When I thought it had gone far enough, and had decided in my own mind not then and there to question him, I asked for a cessation of the speaking, and went and opened the church door.

At once Robert arose and left the church.

Not one word had he spoken to anybody.

Betsy, wife-like, wished immediately to follow him, but Mrs Young persuaded her not to go for a little while. She took the poor frightened creature into the mission house, gave her a cup of tea and something to eat, and what she prized more, some loving sympathetic words. When she did return home, she found that Robert was absent. The children said that he had come in, and, after saying some kind words to them, had taken his gun and ammunition and had gone off hunting. He did not return until the next day, but he had with him a fine deer. This he skinned himself, and taking the two hind quarters, went as usual to the fort, and bartered them for flour, tea and sugar. When he returned to his tent, he handed these things to his wife, and desired her to cook them as usual. After all had been prepared he had all placed before his wife, daughters, and sons. Then, telling them to enjoy the meal, he left the tent. Taking a net, he went out upon the lake in a canoe, and after some time spent in fishing, was seen cooking and eating his catch upon the shore.

Thus he lived for weeks. He was a good hunter, and worked most industriously and successfully. All the game taken, he brought to his wife and children, upon which he insisted that they should feast, while he confined himself to a fish diet; although those caught at that season were far from being the best.

One Saturday evening, as we were standing in the front of our mission home enjoying the splendours of a most magnificent sunset, we saw Robert coming up the trail. As he drew near I accosted him kindly, but it was easy to see that he was in trouble, and that there was "something on his mind." We chatted about various things, and I encouraged him to speak out freely. With a sudden effort he broke loose from his feeling of restraint, and said:

"Missionary, are you going to let me come to the Sacrament of the Lord's Supper to-morrow?"

Four times a year we had this sacramental service, and it was a great event to our native Christians. In answer to his question I replied:

"Why Robert, what is there to cause me to wish to prevent you from coming to the Lord's table?"

Looking at me earnestly, he said:

"There is a good deal. Just think of the way I have treated my wife and daughters!"

"Yes," I said, "I remember that; but I also know how you have been treating them during the last few weeks."

With a face from which the shadows had now fled away, he said quickly:—

"Have you heard anything about that?"

"O yes, Robert," I replied, "I know all about it. I have good eyes and ears, and I have seen and heard how nobly you have redeemed yourself. I am very glad of it. Of course I will welcome you to the Lord's table."

After a little further conversation, I said:

"Tell me, Robert, why did you act so selfishly toward your wife and daughters?"

He just uttered with emphasis the Indian word which means: "Stupidity,"—then after a little pause he quietly added; "But I think I have got over it."

And so he had.

Chapter Fourteen.

Five Indians and a Jack-Knife.


Indian boys dearly love pocket-knives. As they have to make their own bows and arrows, the paddles for their birch canoes, and also the frames for their snow shoes, of course a good knife is a valued possession. In whittling, Indian boys do not push the knife from them, but always draw it toward them. They are very clever in the manufacture of the few things which they require, and are encouraged by their fathers to do their work as neatly as possible. So the better the knife, the better the work which these Indian lads can do, and they are ambitious to possess the very best knife that it is possible for them to obtain; just as the older Indians will give any price within their means for the very best guns that are made. Knowing this love for a good knife, I once used it among a lot of Indian lads, as an incentive to encourage them to sing: as our story will explain.

At one of our Indian villages, where a flourishing mission with its day and Sunday schools exists, the devoted lady teacher said to me on a recent visit:

"I do wish you would do something to encourage our boys to sing. They have good voices, but they seem afraid to use them. If I do succeed in getting one to sing, the others laugh at him, and then there is no more singing that day."

I gladly promised to do what I could; but before I describe the plan adopted, perhaps I would better give some description of these Indians among whom this courageous young lady was living. Their hunting grounds are in the vast region which lies between Lake Winnipeg and Hudson Bay. They are called Saulteaux, and are a subdivision of the great Algonquin family.

Until very recently they lived altogether by hunting and fishing. So ignorant were they, even of the existence of bread, that when the first missionaries, who translated into their language the Lord's prayer, came to the petition, "Give us this day our daily bread," to make it intelligible to them, they had to translate it, "Give us this day something to keep us in life."

They were, and still are very poor. Once the forests abounded in game, and the richest fur-bearing animals, such as the black and silver foxes, otters, beavers, minks, martens and ermines, were caught in large numbers; but incessant huntings have almost annihilated some of these animals, and others are very difficult to find. The lakes once teemed with fish; but the rapid increase of the white population in the north-western states and in Manitoba has so multiplied the demands, that not one quarter as many fish are now caught as formerly.

The result is, that the poor Indians whose sole dependence was on these things, are not as well off as they formerly were, even with the little help which they receive from the government. Hence it is the imperative duty of the missionaries, not only to Christianise them, but to do all they can, in harmony with the government officials, to encourage them to raise cattle, to cultivate what land is available, and to raise those hardy crops which will come to maturity in such a cold northern region.

This was the place; and those were the Indians whose boys the devoted teacher wished me to encourage to sing. The request was made during the celebration of a feast which I was giving them. I had taken out from civilisation such things as flour, tea, sugar, currants, candies; and at four a.m. the Indian women had come to the place appointed and had cooked the cakes etcetera, and made all other needed preparations.

At about ten the people assembled on the bank of the river in front of the church. Everybody came. All were welcome. It was not asked whether they were Christian or pagan. We greeted them all cordially, and treated them alike.

Of the happy incidents of the feast, the glad hours of loving converse, and the religious services held after, we have no room here to write. Suffice it to say, that at about four p.m. the children's hour came, and with them we had a very interesting time. I was delighted with their answers to my many questions, especially with their knowledge of the blessed Book. The girls sang very sweetly, but not much music came from the boys, and so I began at once to act on the request of the teacher.

Knowing, as I have stated, the boys' love for pocket-knives, I went to one of my boxes, and taking out six very good ones, I stood up before the crowd and said:

"Boys, listen to me. I am going to give these six knives to the six boys who will sing the best. And look! While five of them are good two bladed knives, one of them is a splendid four bladed one! Now, I am going to give this best one, to the boy who will sing the best of all!"

Great indeed was the excitement among the Indian lads. Nearly every boy in the audience rushed to the front and the trial began. Indians in their wild state have no music worth preserving, and so in all of our missions, our hymns and songs are translated, and the tunes of civilisation are used. The teacher seated herself at the little organ, and the testing began. They sang such hymns as "Rock of Ages," "Come, thou Fount of every blessing," "Just as I am," "Jesus my all, to heaven is gone," and many others.

The inferior singers were weeded out very rapidly, and sent back to their seats. When the number was reduced to about ten, the work of selection proceeded more slowly; but eventually the number was reduced to six. The question now was, Which of these six was to receive the four-bladed knife? This was not easy to settle. The members of the committee differed very decidedly; so one boy after another was tried, over and over again, and still no unanimous decision could be reached.

While the committee was discussing the matter, five of the boys, seeing our perplexity, took the matter out of our hands and settled it in a way that surprised and delighted us all. These five were fine specimens of Indian lads. They were lithe and strong, and full of life and fun. The sixth boy, Jimmie Jakoos, was a cripple, having one leg which was very much shorter than the other: the result being that he had to use crutches. These five had moved over to one side, and were observed to be excitedly, though quietly, engaged in conversation.

After their brief discussion, one of them sprang up, and looking at me asked:

"Missionary, may I say something?"

"Certainly you may," I replied.

"Well, missionary," he answered, "we five boys have been talking it over, and this is what we think about it. You see we are well and strong. We can chase the rabbit, and partridge, and other game; and then when winter comes, we can skate on the rivers, and lake; but Jimmie is lame, he has a bad leg. He cannot run in the woods. He cannot go skating on the ice. But Jimmie is fond of whittling. He is a good hand at making bows, and arrows, and paddles, and other things, and a fine knife would be just the thing for him. And so we five boys have talked the matter over, and as he is a cripple, we will be very glad if you will give the best knife to Jimmie."

Noble boys! How the people were thrilled at this speech. It electrified me, and filled not only my eyes with tears, but my heart with joy.

I could but think of the past, of the cruelty and intense selfishness of those dark days, when, among both the young and old, everyone was for himself, and the unfortunate, and feeble, were neglected and despised. Now, thanks to the blessed ennobling influences of Christianity, even the boys were catching this Christly spirit, and would spontaneously act in this delightful way.

So to Jimmie was given the four-bladed knife and to the other boys were handed the two-bladed ones; but so pleased was I with the beautiful spirit displayed by them, that I added to the gift a good shirt or jacket as each boy chose.

## Chapter Fifteen.

## The Saulteaux Chieftainess; or, A Searcher after the Truth.

She was a large woman, and as she came into our mission home her conduct was so different from that of the ordinary Indian woman, that I was somewhat prejudiced against her. Generally the Indian women when they enter a house are quiet, and modest, and unobtrusive in their movements; but here stalked in a large woman, who gazed at us with searching glances, and had such decided ways, that I felt disturbed at her presence and soon left the house for a couple of hours in the woods where some of my Indian men were at work.

When I returned, it was with the hope that she had finished her visit and retired. But no, there she was; and it was quite evident that she had come to stay. When my good wife saw my apparent annoyance at this new visitor, she called me to one side and said:

"You must not be annoyed at this woman. She is a chieftainess, and the daughter of a chief. Her husband was a chief, and when he died, she, at the request of her people, took his position, and has maintained it ever since."

She had heard from some fur-hunters about our having come to live in the land of the Saulteaux. She had also heard of the wonderful book we had, which was the word of the Great Spirit; and this too, had excited her curiosity. She had listened to these rumours with incredulity and did not believe them; but as they increased, her curiosity was so excited, that she resolved at length to find out for herself if these things were true, and had actually come many days journey to investigate for herself. Here she was, thoroughly installed in our little home, and I, at first, much prejudiced against her on account of her decided emphatic sort of way.

I sat down beside her, and had her tell me her story. She was indeed a clever woman, and was full of anxiety to learn if what she had heard were true. She was an anxious inquirer after truth, literally insatiable in her curiosity, and in her desire to learn all she could. She could talk morning, noon and night, and would keep one of us busy answering her questions all the time she was not sleeping or eating.

She stayed with us about two weeks, and then returned to her people; meanwhile attending every religious service, and receiving many lessons in divine truth. The simple plan of salvation was explained to her, and she was taught how to pray.

Ere she went away, I said to her: Now you are going back home, and I want to say something to you. You must try to remember what we have said about the loving Father, and His beloved Son. You must try to pray every day to Him, and you must try to love Him and keep all of His commands.

"Now one of these commands is, 'Remember the Sabbath day to keep it holy.' Christians keep one day in seven, and you say that your people desire to be Christians; and I believe you. We want you to be a Christian in everything, and so we want you to remember this among the other commandments. To help you in this matter, I am going to give you this big sheet of paper and pencil, and you will mark each day as it goes by."

So starting her on Monday, I showed her how to mark the days in this way:—111111. "Those six are your days, in which to hunt and fish and attend to all your duties as a chieftainess. Look after all your affairs on those six days; then, when the seventh day comes, make a big mark in this way:—

"This mark is for God's day. Leave your gun and net on that day, and do not go hunting or fishing: it is the day of rest and worship. Make all preparations for it on the day before. See that you have plenty of food captured, and wood cut, so that when the day of God chines, you will not have to work or hunt or fish. On that day think much about the Great Spirit, and pray much to your loving father who sees and hears you all the time, and who is well pleased if we keep His day and worship Him upon it."

Ere she left, she pleaded earnestly with me to come and visit her and her tribe, and preach to them, and explain the way of the Great Book. My engagements were very many but finding that I could crowd in a visit, I said:

"When the eagle-moon is filling out listen for the ringing of the missionary's sleigh-bells, for then will he be coming to see you and your people with his dog-train and guide."

My programme of engagements was so great, that it was about six months ere I could make the promised visit. So when the eagle moon came—which is February—I harnessed up my dogs, and taking one of my experienced guides and a couple of dog-drivers, started for the far-off land of Ookemasis.

We were about two weeks on the journey. It was one of the most dangerous and toilsome I ever undertook. We often had to travel along on the narrow ledges of ice that overhung the rapid waters of the great river. Sometimes our dog-sleds would whirl round on the ice and we come very near falling off into the dark cold waters. This was much more dangerous from the fact, that much of the travelling had to be done by night for the dazzling rays of the sun during the daytime rendered us so liable to the terrible snow-blindness, which is such a painful disease. However, we persevered, and by daylight when possible, and by night when we could do no better, pushed on, and at last reached our destination.

The last six miles of the journey lay across a frozen lake on the farther shore of which was the village of the chieftainess. When not more than half way across the lake, the sharp eyes of those on the lookout, detected our coming, whereupon great excitement prevailed in the village. Never, it seemed, was there a happier woman than Ookemasis. She received us with a wondrous welcome, and in emphatic ways expressed her gratitude and joy. Already when we arrived, the feast of welcome was being prepared. When she was certain that it was the missionary, she had taken down from a staging some heads of reindeer, and, after singeing off the hair and chopping them into great chunks, had put them into a big pot to boil.

After the warm welcome, we were escorted to a large tent to wait until dinner was ready. As she had no tea, I gave her a quantity much to her delight. So excited was she, that she kept running into the tent to tell me how great was her joy, that at length the man and the Book had come to her people. When dinner was ready, she escorted me and my attendants out to it. A spot had been cleaned away, in the centre of which, on a big dish, was a large pile of pieces of reindeer heads. Around were a number of tin cups filled with hot strong tea. Her invitations had been limited to the number of tin cups she could muster. She placed me at her left, and her chief next in authority to herself, on her right. My guide and dog-drivers were next to me on my left, and the circle was completed with other Indian men. She was the only woman in the circle as soon as we were seated on the ground, some of the men at once seized hold of a piece of meat, and drawing their hunting knives, were about to begin their dinners:

"Stop," said I. "Wait a minute. You are all going to be Christians, and one thing Christians do, is to ask a blessing upon their food. The Great Spirit gives us all the good things, and we must thank Him for them. So now shut your eyes, and I will ask the blessing."

Every eye was closed as I asked a blessing of several sentences. When I had finished, I said "Amen" and of course opened my own eyes. To my amazement and amusement, every eye, except those of my own Indian attendants, was still closed. "Open your eyes," I said. "Amen, here means, open your eye. It has some other meanings, but that will do here."

Then we went at our dinners. There were no plates or forks, only our hunting knives. Every one, including the missionary, took up a piece of the well-cooked meat in his left hand, and began whittling off his dinner with his knife. My friend, the chieftainess, had large, strong and not very clean hands. But she cared not for that. She grabbed up a large piece of juicy meat, into which her hand almost sank, and cut and tore off the savoury bits with great delight. Then she flung it on the ground and took a good drink of the tea; and then seizing hold of the meat tore at it again with great satisfaction. Suddenly she dropped it again upon

the ground, and, plunging her greasy hand into the bosom
of her dress, said:

"O, missionary, I want you to see how I have tried to keep
the record of the praying day." So out of the bosom of her
dress she drew a greasy dirty paper, which at first I did not
recognise as the large clean sheet I had given her.

"Here, look," she said, "see how I have tried to keep the
record of the praying day!"

With much interest, I examined it, and found, that during
all those six months, she had faithfully kept the record.
There it was; the right day for all that long period. Then she
went on to tell me of all her experiences. She said, that
some days when she was in her wigwam trying to think of
the Great Spirit and of His Son, and was trying to pray to
Him, a boy would rush in and say:

"Ookemasis, there is a big reindeer out in the ravine, I am
sure you can shoot it."

"But I would say, 'No. This is the praying day and I cannot
fish or shoot on this day.' So I have never gone hunting or
fishing on the praying day. I just try to think of the Great
Spirit, my Father, and to pray and talk to Him, and have
Him talk to me."

Of course I spoke kind and encouraging words to her, and
she was very happy indeed to hear them.

Then she put back the dirty paper, and reaching down to
the ground again seized hold of her big piece of meat.
Looking at mine, a bony bit which I had selected because I

could hold it a little more easily while I carved it, she
shouted out:

"Your piece of meat is a very poor one, mine is a very good
piece," and before I could realise what she was about, she
exchanged the pieces. Of course I could do nothing but
accept it, with thanks. I had to approve of the motive, even
if I did not applaud the deed. It was an act of kindness that
we are not all educated up to.

After the dinner we had a religious service that lasted until
supper time. Then, after a good supper of fish, we had
another service, that lasted until midnight. Then she put me
in charge of one of her Indians who had a large wigwam.
With him my Indians and I spent the night. There were only
twenty-two of us sleeping around the fire in the centre.

I remained with them for a number of days, and since then,
they have all given up paganism, and have become good
earnest Christian people.

Chapter Sixteen.

Big Tom.

His full name was Mamanowatum, which means, "O be joyful." He was a big man, almost gigantic, and generally slow in his movements, except when on the trail. When he arose to address an assembly, either in council, or church, he got up by inches, and seemed to rest between. But when he was up, and began to talk, he had something to say that was worthy of attention.

Our first introduction to him was in 1868. He was the guide and steersman of the Hudson Bay inland boat, in which my wife and I travelled from Fort Garry, on the Red River of the North, to Norway House, situated on Playgreen Lake, beyond the northern extremity of Lake Winnipeg.

At this time Big Tom, as he was called by everybody, had been an earnest Christian for several years. Earlier missionaries had preceded us, and among the Indian converts was this godly man, about whom it is a pleasure to write. We both took to him at once. He was one of nature's noblemen. While pleased with his kindly considerate ways, we admired the skill and ability with which he managed the little boat on such a stormy lake.

The long and dangerous journey was of about four hundred miles and occupied us for about fourteen days. Big Tom steered our boat with a long oar, which he used as a rudder. The principal propelling power of these boats, is the long strong oars, manned by the Indian crews. We had in our boat eight good oarsmen, and the vigour and endurance of these men was a matter of constant admiration. When head winds prevailed, or we were in the midst of calm, hour sifter hour these faithful men toiled on at their oars, as diligently as ever did any galley slave. A favouring breeze, even if it turned into a dangerous gale, was ever welcomed, as it gave the men a rest from their slavish work.

As soon as the wind was favourable the cheery cry of:

"Meyoo-nootin," (Fair wind,) from the guide,—or as was the cry on this trip, "Souway-nas," (South wind,)— gladdened every heart. At once there was great activity. The oars were hauled in, and the mast which had been lashed to the side of the boat, was quickly placed in position. Ropes were speedily arranged, the big square sail was hoisted, and on we sped before the favouring breeze.

With the rising of the wind, generally came the great waves; and the most careful steering on the part of Big Tom was necessary to keep our heavily laden boat from plunging her prow into foam-covered billows. It was a pleasure to observe the watchful care of this cautious steersman, as well as to see the strength and quickness with which he managed our little boat when great waves seemed about to sweep over us. His courteous ways won our respect, while his ability as a steersman commanded our admiration.

He did all that he could to make our trip, which had many drawbacks, as comfortable and as enjoyable as possible. It was not very comfortable to have a great struggling ox on board, very close to the place where we had to sit. Sometimes, as the boat was tossed on the waves, his head was over one side of the little craft; and then shortly after, his tail was over the other side.

Every night where we camped on the shore. Big Tom
gathered bundles of fragrant grass, part of which he gave
the ox as provender, and with the rest he endeavoured to
make our surroundings more comfortable and inviting. He
regretted, perhaps as much as we did, our having to travel
so long a time with this great ox so close to us; and yet ere
we reached the end of our journey, it seemed almost a
certainty, that what we had considered an unmitigated
nuisance, had been our salvation. One night, in our anxiety
to push on, the Indians decided not to go ashore and camp,
but to sail on all night as the wind was favourable. During
the small hours the wind increased almost to a gale, while
dark clouds obscured nearly every star. Big Tom—hero
that he was—stuck to his post and, nobly aided by his
experienced Indians, under close-reefed sail, sped rapidly
on in the gloom. The missionary and his wife were sleeping
in their camp bed, which had been spread out at the feet of
the steersman; and just beyond us, lying down at our feet,
was the great ox. Suddenly the boat was thrown on its side,
and came to a standstill. For a time there was great
excitement, and the shouting of orders by the usually quiet
Indians, about equalled the raging of the storm.

With great presence of mind. Big Tom instantly lowered
the sail, thus saving us from a complete upset. It was found
that we had run on the sloping side of a smooth submerged
granite rock. Fortunate indeed was it for us that our boat
was well ballasted by its cargo, and that the heaviest item
was the ox. The unanimous opinion of the Indians was, that
his great weight saved us from a capsize. By careful
management the boat was released from its perilous
position uninjured, and the adventurous journey resumed.

After this exciting adventure. Big Tom decided that there
must be no more night travelling. So from early dawn until

late at night we hurried on, encamping each evening in some favourable spot upon the shore.

The camp-fire, generously supplied with fuel from the great forests so near, lit up the swarthy features of our stalwart men, some of whom were engaged in preparing the evening meal, while others, in picturesque groups, were otherwise occupied. This hearty evening meal was enjoyed by all.

Shortly after, we all assembled for our evening devotions. Some additional logs thrown upon our camp-fire so brightened it up, that all who wished could easily follow the reading of the lesson in their own Testaments and use their own hymn-books in the service of song. The memories of some of those religious services are very precious. Still can we hear Big Tom's deep rich voice reading in his musical Cree language:

"Weya Muneto a ispeeche saketapun uske, ke niakew oo pauko-Koosisana, piko una tapwatowayitche numaweya oo ga nissewunatissety, maka oo ga ayaty kakeka pimatissewin." Which is the translation of that matchless verse, the sixteenth of the third chapter of Saint John's Gospel.

Then after the chapter was read, an appropriate hymn would be sung. The Indians have but little music of their own, and less poetry that can be made available for religious worship. The result is, that the missionaries and teachers have already translated over four hundred of our choicest hymns into the Indian language, and use with them the tunes with which they have been generally associated. Upon the occasion to which we refer, it did seem sweet and appropriate to us to sing, even if in another language, the favourite evening hymn:

"Glory to thee my God this night,

For all the blessings of the light;

Keep me, O keep me King of kings,

Beneath thine own almighty wings."

When our evening hymn had been sung, we knelt reverently upon the rocks, while Big Tom, or some other godly Indian, led us in prayer, followed by one or two others. Then sweet rest was ours, until the early dawn. A sharp call, to which all promptly responded, was followed by a hasty breakfast, and earnest prayers, and then the journey was resumed.

Two Sabbaths were spent on this journey. To our Christian Indians, the Sabbath was indeed a much prized blessing. By scripturally using it as a day of rest and religious worship, and not as a day of dissipation, they were physically, as well as spiritually, invigorated; and thus able to do much better work. We had, in addition to the morning and evening prayers, two delightful religious services in both the Indian and English languages. The intervals between were spent in reading the Book and some sweet song services.

As the years rolled on, with their varied duties, we ever found in Big Tom, a most valued and trusted assistant. His noble consistent life, made him a benediction, to both whites and Indians. If disputes arose, and arbitration was necessary, it was Big Tom who was first thought of as an arbitrator; and we cannot recall an instance where his decision was rejected.

He was a great hunter in his day, and many were the stories afloat of his skill and prowess. For years he held the record of being the best moose hunter in the village. The moose, although the largest of the deer tribe, and of an ungainly appearance, can move through the forest with great rapidity. It never gallops like other deer, but swings along on a pacing trot, at a rate, and with an endurance that would soon leave the swiftest horse behind. Its head is freighted with great broad horns of enormous dimensions and weight, and yet among the dense trees, it can, when alarmed, move so swiftly, that the fleetest hunter is soon left far in the rear. Its sight is not equal to that of some other of the deer species; but nature has given it the most acute powers of hearing and of scent. From Big Tom and others we have heard it stated, that even when a fierce November storm was raging in the woods, with trees swaying to and fro, and branches crashing against each other and breaking in the gale, if the incautious hunter, hundreds of yards away, happened to step on a small dry twig that snapped under his foot, the moose at once detected the sound and was off like an arrow, never stopping for many miles.

Of Big Tom's skill as a hunter, we have nothing more to record at present; but here we wish to put on record an instance of his self-abnegation, which beautifully reveals the disinterested character of the man, and shows what was the heart's ambition.

For many generations these American Indians have been divided into tribes. Many and diverse are their languages; but numbers of their customs and methods of government are similar. In all the tribes chiefs governed who had more or less authority. In some, the honour was hereditary; in others, not so; although in the latter the son of the chief, if he were at all suitable, had the best chance of being appointed in his father's place. When the Canadian government made treaties with the Indians of the great north-west, it ever acknowledged the authority of the chiefs; and through them, today still transacts all business with the tribes. For some time before the treaty was made with the northern Crees, the office of chieftainship had fallen into abeyance. When word arrived that the government was about to enter into treaty with them, and wished to know who was their chief, there was a good deal of excitement. The Dominion government has been very honourable in its treatment of the Indians, and in the respect which it has paid to the chiefs of this naturally sensitive people, whose allowances have been silver medals, fine clothes, and extra gratuities, both in money and supplies. Of course there was excitement among the Crees at the prospect of great political changes. Councils were frequent, and many pipes were smoked in wigwams and beside camp-fires over the matter. Various names were discussed, and sons and grandsons were brought forward, only to be rejected one after another. Big Tom took but little interest in these proceedings, and attended but few councils. One day to his surprise, while at work in his garden, he was waited upon by a deputation of Indians and informed that he was urgently needed at the council house. Here in full council he was told that he was the choice of the people, and that they wanted him to be their chief—to wear the silver medal with the face of the Great Mother (the Queen) upon it, and to be their voice to speak to the Queen's representative, (the Governor), on all matters that referred to the happiness and welfare of the tribe.

I had been informed of the decision of the people, and had accepted an invitation to be present at the council when Big Tom was to be appointed. In other days, I had attended conventions among my white friends, and there had observed the readiness with which proffered honours, political and ecclesiastical, were accepted. Here, however, was a surprise in store for us; an exception to the general rule, so marvellous that it is worth pondering.

When the office of chief was offered to him, the big man, who looked every inch a chief, instead of accepting the position at once, became deeply affected, and seemed utterly unable to make any suitable reply. He tried, we thought, to express his thanks for the great honour; but all he really did was in broken words to ask for an adjournment of the council until the next day. While disappointed at the adjournment, I was pleased at the thought that Big Tom, taken unawares, had felt that he could not give the oration which the occasion demanded, and so had asked for time to get his thoughts in order, when he would give us a speech worthy of the great event; for Big Tom was a speaker of no mean order, although rather slow until he warmed up to his subject.

On the reassembling of the council, we were all there, eager to hear an Indian oration under the best auspices. It was a speech, calm, eloquent, delightful; but how different from what had been expected. What a chance was here for an ambitious, aspiring man! How he could have talked about himself; what he had done, and what he was going to do! But in Big Tom's address there was nothing of the kind. Quietly and modestly he talked, warming up as he proceeded. The only brief report I have of his address is the following, and it fails to do justice to the occasion or to the man:

"Long ago when the missionaries came and preached to us, for a time we refused to listen to them, and would not become Christians. Then, after a while, many of us who had been in darkness, began to feel in our hearts, that what they told us was for our good; and so we accepted these things, and they have done us good. When I got the assurance in my heart that I was a child of God, and had a soul that should live forever, I found, that in working out this salvation, I had something great to live for. To do this was the great object of my life. By and by I married, and then, as my family increased and began to grow up around me, I found I had another object for which to live—to help its members along in the way to heaven, as well as to work for their comfort here.

"Then, after a while, the missionary gave me the charge of a class. We were to meet, and talk together about our souls, and God's love for us, and to do all we could to help each other to the better land. To do my duty as the leader was a great and an important work. While attending to these duties, I found I had another object for which to live. These three things,—my own soul's salvation; the salvation of my family; to do all I can to help and encourage the members of my class to be true and faithful to Him,—are uppermost in my heart.

"I am thankful for your confidence in me, in asking me to be your chief. I know it is a great honour; but I see it will have many responsibilities, and, that whoever has the position, will have to attend to many other things than those which I have set my mind upon. So you must appoint some one else; for, with those three things I cannot let anything else interfere. I thank you, my brothers, and love you all."

Noble, disinterested Big Tom! As I listened to him while he thus talked, I was prouder of him than ever; and I thanked

God for the conversion of such men from paganism to Christianity, and for the development in their hearts and lives of such noble qualities and virtues.

Made in the USA
Monee, IL
24 September 2024

66507029R00095